Learning how to interpret themes and inspiration in your own individual way can lead to wonderfully varied artworks. This stunning collection showcases the work produced by renowned textile artists Els van Baarle and Cherilyn Martin, and explores how – even when working from the same starting point – textile art can produce myriad interpretations of shape, form, colour and technique.

Whatever your preferred technique, whether you work with dyes, embroidery, found objects or collage, Els and Cherilyn teach you how to draw inspiration from your memory and motifs, as well as your surroundings. The book is illustrated throughout with inspirational details of their work, along with step-by-step instructions and tips. They demonstrate a variety of methods for you to apply to your own artworks – including transfers, controlled rusting, wax-resist dyeing techniques, bookbinding, surface rubbings, encaustic collages and hand-embroidered portraits – to unleash your creativity.

INTERPRETING THEMES
IN TEXTILE ART

Els van Baarle and
Cherilyn Martin

BATSFORD

First published in the United Kingdom in 2017 by
Batsford
43 Great Ormond Street
London WC1N 3HZ

An imprint of Pavilion Books Company Ltd

Volume © Batsford, 2017
Text and illustrations © Els van Baarle and Cherilyn Martin, 2017

The moral rights of the authors have been asserted.

All rights reserved. No part of this publication may be reproduced,
stored in a retrieval system, or transmitted in any form or by any means,
electronic, mechanical, photocopying, recording or otherwise, without
the prior written permission of the copyright owner.

ISBN: 9781849944366

A CIP catalogue record for this book is available from the British Library.

10 9 8 7 6 5 4 3 2 1

Reproduction by Mission Productions Ltd, Hong Kong
Printed and bound by Toppan Leefung, China

This book can be ordered direct from the publisher
at the website: www.pavilionbooks.com, or try your local bookshop.

Contents

Foreword	4
Complementary yet Individual	6
Introduction	9
1. The Creative Process	10
2. Graven Images	28
3. Walls	44
4. Pompeii	58
5. Yesterday is History	74
6. Book as Object	90
7. Articles in Everyday Use	108
Materials	124
Suppliers	125
Further Reading	126
Index	127

Foreword

The fibre art of Els van Baarle (NL) and Cherilyn Martin (UK/NL) spans more than two and a half decades and it represents a love affair with colour, images and textures on cloth, paper and other mixed media. Both have their own signature styles but when they co-exhibit, there is a natural synergy between their works that is evident – each individual envisions a conceptual theme that complements the artwork of the other arist.

I had known of Els's and Cherilyn's art practice for many years. In 2009 I met Els when she was a participating artist in the exhibition that I curated, 'ArtCloth: Engaging New Visions', which toured Australia until 2011. In September of 2011 I was delighted to meet both Els and Cherilyn who, along with myself, were workshop tutors at a five-day textile/fibre conference, 'Cloth Arts @ Hunters Hill, Sydney', organised by Glenys Mann of Fibre Arts Australia. Our paths crossed once again in October 2014 when I opened the exhibition, 'Memory Cloth – Rememberings in Textile' by four internationally renowned textile artists – Els van Baarle, Cherilyn Martin, Cas Holmes and Glenys Mann at the Museum de Kantfabriek in Horst, the Netherlands. Els and Cherilyn have exhibited and given workshops in Europe, North America and Australasia, so they are well known across a myriad of artistic landscapes. Art-making as well as informing and teaching the current and next generation of artistic practitioners ensures that the techniques they have mastered and the concepts that they have explored will linger beyond their own generation.

Art can be created out of ignorance and by chance, but this book aims far higher. It aims to link your life experiences, your knowledge, your exploration of language, myths, cultures, symbols and motifs to your ability using fibre, and by fibre, I am using the broadest definition possible – from cloth to paper to thread. Of course, in the process, colour and texture are an integral part of the development of a concept.

You need to be aware of all the rules and so the first chapter gives you a comprehensive compositional and optical road map, not to inhibit your creative processes but rather to make you conscious of which rule(s) you choose to break. To get the effect you have to know the cause! Imagery on fibre can be made incredibly smooth and flat, as were the painted and printed images created by Pop Artists such as Roy Lichtenstein in *Drowning Girl* (1963). On the other hand, fibre art can have texture, which gives it an extra dimensionality. Chapter 2 is inspired by inscriptions and gravestone imagery and explores this dimensionality from the rubbing process to embroidery, and the use of crayons and transfer paints. The fascination with images, typography and the texture that exposed walls offer has been with us since the dawn of time, from the huntsman's marks made on cave walls, to drawings and obscenities carved on clay found in the excavations of Pompeii, to modern-day graffiti and the urban, architectural landscapes that surround us. Both artists give valuable insights into their own personal interpretations and working methodologies, which incorporate these themes in Chapter 3. Chapter 3's fascination is continued with the walls of Pompeii in Chapter 4, where it is placed in a historical and cultural setting. Although the voices of the dead can no longer be heard, their endeavours – such as their architecture, the way they lived, how they decorated, and their cultural mores – enables a themed artistic exploration in today's world using techniques and ideas in fibre art. Life experiences play an important part in pursuing artistic endeavours. Can you project artistically 'grief' because of a loss, or wondrous excitement because of a birth? Memory plays a part in interpreting these emotional responses as we all accumulate personalised, unique imagery, experiences and sensations during our lifetimes. Preserving memory when it comes to artistic translation can be difficult. Chapter 5 gives two in-depth perspectives on how our sensory track can be mastered to create rich visual stories about personal memories. Books may be becoming electronic but their soul lies within fibre and not in a projected computer language. The smell of the binder, the texture of the paper and the visual concept that unfolds before us, makes us want to see, feel and read and so know the art form. Chapter 6 gives practical insights with respect to technique in order to make a three-dimensional, readable and viewable art form. Art can be made from found objects and everyday materials. For example, El Anatsui is an African artist who works with repurposed materials including wood, aluminium printing plates, tin boxes and liquor bottle tops. Chapter 7 explores the use of common found objects and how they can be incorporated into fibre artworks employing numerous surface-design techniques and concepts.

This book is special since it gives practical insights into creating complex imagery and texture using a large range of fibre material. The authors want to arouse your curiosity, and engage you in an artistic conversation where you, the reader, will understand what concepts and techniques in fibre art will work for your artistic expression. Sure you need to know the fundamentals, but in learning and exploring your art using this book you have fun as well!

I know you will enjoy this book as much as I have.

Marie-Therese Wisniowski
Studio Artist and Founder of Art Quill Studio and Art Quill & Co. Pty. Ltd.
Former Co-Editor *Textile Fibre Forum* art magazine
Casual Lecturer, Faculty of Education and Arts, The University of Newcastle, NSW, Australia

Complementary yet individual

Throughout the centuries there has been interaction between artists. Mutual respect, interest and admiration for other artists' work has a positive effect. It becomes even more interesting when the themes they choose to work in parallel on a shared theme.

Two textile artists, Els van Baarle (NL) and Cherilyn Martin (UK/NL), met more than twenty-five years ago. Although they both have an individual approach to their work, a special bond was forged between them, fuelled by their intense interest in the same topics: the past, the passage of time, ancient cultures and marks left by Man are all subjects about which they are both passionate.

Both artists immerse themselves in their chosen themes, sometimes spending several years on the same subject. Consequently, works have evolved that are mature and have depth and meaning. Their interaction has culminated in several distinct exhibitions being shown both nationally and internationally.

The varied work of both these renowned artists is linked through the introspective interpretation of their theme.

About the artists

Above: *Detail of Aardappel II*, Els van Baarl, 20 x 220cm (8 x 86½in). Two layers of silk and cotton, wax, dye, print.

Readers will be inspired as they immerse themselves in the art of Els van Baarle and Cherilyn Martin. Each themed exhibition they have worked on together has the subtitle: 'Two visions on a theme' and it is always fascinating to see how two established artists tackle the same subject.

Els van Baarle www.elsvanbaarle.com

- Textile artist specialising in contemporary batik, surface design and mixed media
- Member of Steek Plus www.steekplus.nl
- Windkracht 10 www.windkrachttien.blogspot.com

Cherilyn Martin www.cherilynmartin.com

- Textile artist specialising in mixed media, experimental quilting and embroidery
- Member of Quilt Art www.quiltart.eu
- Windkracht 10 www.windkrachttien.blogspot.com

Both artists are members of IAPMA (International Association of Hand Papermakers and Paper Artists) www.iapma.info

They are internationally renowned tutors with experience of teaching in the USA, Australia, New Zealand, Canada and throughout Europe.

Above: *Memory Cloth #5*, 110 x 110cm (43 x 43in), Cherilyn Martin. German *Paradekissen*, rusting, screen printing, machine stitching.

How to use this book

Most artists have lots of ideas for their work – sometimes too many – so that they can no longer see the wood for the trees. This book is intended to give all artists a helping hand by showing the approach adopted by Cherilyn Martin and Els van Baarle. The concept 'Two visions on a theme' is at the heart of this book. Both artists show how they work individually and have their own vision and way of developing a commonly chosen theme.

Through regular contact each artist learns about the other's ideas and their way of developing the theme. This is not true collaboration in the sense of working together on one piece of work, but rather each artist makes her own way along the same path. This form of collaboration strengthens their approach.

The hope is that by showing Cherilyn's and Els's individual interpretations of the themes the reader will be encouraged to develop their own interpretation.

The content of work has always been important to Cherilyn and Els; introspection, life experiences and personal interpretations are present in all of their textile art. They do not strive to make decorative pieces, but to produce work which is autonomous and has meaning. They hope to encourage the reader to adapt this same approach, and to develop work beyond technique and materials.

Cherilyn and Els both love the meditative processes of hand embroidery and layering with wax and dye because they offer time for reflection. Working on a theme forces you to focus longer on one topic, so that it becomes impossible to be satisfied with just one solution.

By in-depth exploration of the subject matter, by establishing a link with art history and other cultures, horizons are broadened and new possibilities emerge. Dedicating time to research leads to enrichment of the work.

Knowledge of the elements and principles of design can be a great help when confronted with decision-making during the process of creating. However, one's own input and intuition should not be underestimated. Be aware of the rules but have the courage to break them on the journey to developing a visual language of your own.

Learn the rules like a pro, so you can break them as an artist.
Pablo Picasso

CHAPTER 1

THE CREATIVE PROCESS

Previous page: *Duet,*
Els van Baarle.
Batik on cotton.

Self-awareness is an essential part of understanding your creativity. Questioning who you are and what makes you different from others is the first step on the path to self-discovery. There are three questions you could consider:

- *Who am I?* Analyse your character, for example, what are your strong points, are you confident or self-doubting, are you spontaneous or do you consider things carefully before acting, are you determined?
- *What am I capable of?* List not only what you can do in the sense of making creative work, but also consider questions such as, whether you are able to organise yourself, work independently, make choices.
- *What do I want to achieve?* What are your goals, are they realistic, are they achievable? Do you want to make work essentially for yourself or do you want to gain recognition? Is your work a hobby or do you want to achieve professional status?

The answers to these questions may help you to discover more about yourself and where you actually stand at this moment in time. Reflect on your answers and decide whether you need to change something in your approach to your work. You may even decide to concentrate on improving skills that will help you promote yourself and consequently your work.

Finding your inner voice is fundamental to creating and developing individual, non-derivative work.

Phases in the creative process

There are several phases in the creative process that can help you on your creative journey:

Inspiration

New ideas can be generated by doing research into a selected topic. This should be a time of carefree investigation into areas of interest, without the pressure of deciding on what the finished product should be. Read more about this phase on page 14, 'Choosing a theme'.

Gestation

Leave your ideas to settle for a while so that you can return to them with a fresh mind. Then it will be easier to sift information, enabling you to discard less important data and to choose the most meaningful ideas. This prevents you from being carried away with a superficial idea, which perhaps seemed exciting at the time.

Fruition

Once you have decided on your theme it is time to realise your ideas. Making a piece of work involves the coming together of ideas, materials and technique, and choices have to be made at each stage of the process. You will have to make decisions about the materials you will work with and which techniques you will use. The size of the work is important, as well as the choice of whether to work in two or three dimensions, for example.

Assessment

On completion of a piece of work it is important to evaluate the process and the result. Does your work live up to your expectations? Are there other avenues you could explore? Make a positive critique of your work and look for ways to improve on both the idea and the realisation. One idea should lead to another.

You shouldn't be too disappointed with the results – remember, when creating art you are always in search of that elusive masterpiece. Also, when you are overly satisfied with the results, it is very difficult to move forward.

Creativity takes courage.
Henri Matisse

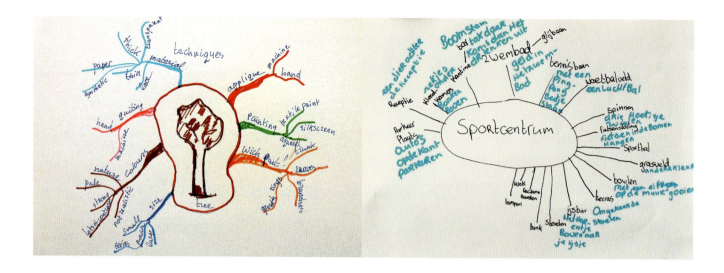

Choosing a theme

It is essential to examine your personal interests in order to make the right choice of theme. You should find the theme inspiring and intriguing – something you are driven to explore in depth. To help understand more about how you can approach developing your theme, mind mapping can be a particularly useful tool.

Above left: A mind map on the theme of trees by Els van Baarle.

Above right: A mind map drawn by Dutch elementary school children.

Mind mapping

After you have chosen a theme, you will soon discover that are so many (perhaps too many) different ways to achieve your finished product. This is confusing, and it makes the start very difficult. You will have to make choices.

Most people make notes in vertical lists, like shopping lists. Another method is to make a mind map. This method was developed by the English psychologist Tony Buzan, and is widely used in schools, companies and among artists.

Our brains are very capable of receiving information through pattern making. We tend to remember an image better than a line with words. In his book *Use Your Head* Tony Buzan writes: 'the brain is capable of infinitely more complex tasks than has been thought'.

How to create a mind map:
- Use a large blank piece of paper.
- Start by placing an image from your theme in the centre.
- Draw different-colour branches from the centre, using words and images.

14 | The Creative Process

- Just make associations. Draw whatever pops up in your mind, and do not hesitate to include silly things!
- On thicker branches write your more important definitions or ideas.
- From each branch smaller branches can be drawn. Each word has its own branch.
- By using different colours you will remember the pattern better.
- Let the map grow organically: there is no right or wrong, just a wealth of ideas.
- Let the map force you to think 'out of the box', beyond boundaries.
- As the next step, look at your map, and choose one word or image to develop your idea further.
- Make a new mind map using that chosen word/image.
- In this way you are narrowing down the possibilities for your idea.
- As before, remember to let your mind be free, and don't be afraid to write 'odd' ideas.

There are two mind maps illustrated above, one with the common words connected to the subject, while the second mind map narrows an idea down to the possibility of using a tree in a textile work. With mind mapping you can also explore and make decisions about the materials and colours you associate with the theme. As mentioned before, the ideas generated by researching your theme should offer enough inspiration for long-term exploration.

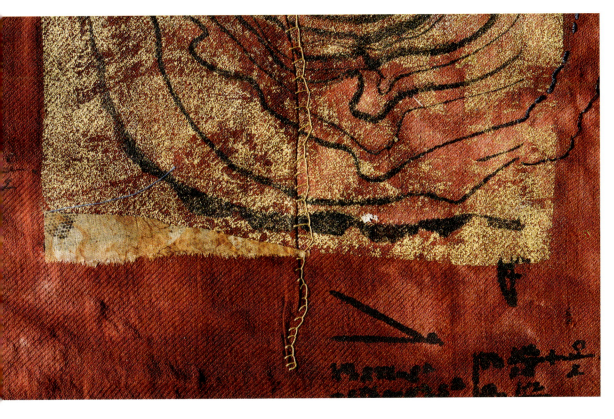

Left: *Trees* (detail) 40 x 135cm (15½ x 53in), Els van Baarle. Wool, silk, wax, dye, print. Work developed from the mind map opposite, based on the image of a tree and its growth-rings.

The Creative Process | 15

Making a start

When you have chosen your theme, it is very important to do as much visual research into your subject matter as possible. Using the internet to collect images and information is an easy option and something that can be done when it most suits you.

Photography is an invaluable aid to your research: always have your camera (or the camera on your mobile phone) at hand.

Using a sketchbook is also vital. Sketching in situ focuses the eye and encourages you to look in detail at the subject matter. Some people say they cannot draw, but the following tips will help you make useful sketches.

- Colour pages before you go on location, so that you are not confronted with the vastness of a white page when you begin.
- Make collages on pages, so that you can sketch into them.
- Start by introducing the colour palette you associate with your theme.

Above left: Sketchbook page, Cherilyn Martin.

Above right: Sketch with twigs and ink, Cherilyn Martin.

Visual inspiration

Accept that there are more ways of drawing than simply rendering a realistic interpretation. Your drawing doesn't need to be exact – that's what cameras are for. Focus on small details, using simple lines to give the impression of shapes or landscape.

16 | The Creative Process

Above: Design sheet, Cherilyn Martin.

Drawing is mark making, so you can use a variety of 'tools' to work with, not just a pencil or pen. When working in situ you can pick up sticks and twigs, dip them in paint or ink and use them to draw with. Immediately the quality of line takes on new meaning.

Think about using earth or sand as colouring agents to give the impression of the area you are working in. When you feel you have collected enough visual information as inspiration, you can then begin to think about your materials and the form the work will take.

Making samples with your materials is an essential part of the process, as discovering what you can do with a material is invaluable.

At this stage some artists work spontaneously from the materials they have selected, exploring their qualities and relying on the materials to lead them, combined, of course, with the ideas developed during their research. Other artists prefer to have a clear idea of where they are going; by creating a design sheet much of their research is displayed logically showing colour palettes, material choices and samples of techniques, as shown above.

It is important you decide which approach is most suited to you. It is also essential to have some knowledge of the elements and principles of design when creating work. In this book we are giving special attention to composition and colour.

The Creative Process | 17

Composition

Composition is the ordering of visual elements according to the principles of design. This is a strategy that helps artists create structure within the visual field. A strong composition is essential to a successful piece of work.

Basic elements of design are: line, shape/form, space, colour, value and texture.

Elements of design in textiles

Elements are arranged in a composition according to the principles of design. How these elements are arranged affects the idea the artist is trying to convey and also the viewer's perception of the work. These principles include: proportion, focus, balance, contrast and movement to name but a few. There is much discussion among artists about which subjects belong under which heading. Some profess that pattern, for example, is an element, while others are convinced that it is a principle.

Proportion

Proportion refers to the relative size and scale of the various elements within a work. Here are the traditional methods used to achieve successful proportions in a composition:

The golden mean

Classical Greek architecture was based on the golden rectangle, which the Greeks constructed using the ratio 1:1.61, believing it to contain the most mathematically pleasing proportions. It was later used by Renaissance painters, including Leonardo da Vinci, and continues to be employed today by some architects and artists.

The Fibonacci sequence

The Fibonacci sequence, 1, 1, 2, 3, 5, 8, 13, 21, expresses the golden mean and can be found in nature, in the spiralling patterns of sunflower seeds on the seed head, in the seedpods of pine cones, in nautilus shells and many other natural structures.

Right: Fibonacci spiral in a collage composition.

Far right: Rule of thirds in a collage composition.

The rule of thirds

This rule is very easy to apply in composition. The image is divided by two equally spaced vertical lines and two horizontal lines. When taking a photograph you can activate a display with this grid on both your digital camera and mobile-phone screens. This will help you make a good photographic composition. A composition becomes more exciting when important elements of the design, such as a focal point, are placed along these lines and at their intersections (known as power points).

Focal point

Right: *Arte Factum*, 20 x 20 x 3cm (8 x 8 x 1¼1in), Cherilyn Martin. Encaustic and paper collage. In this composition the two main focal elements are placed according to this rule of thirds.

The focal point is a point of emphasis within a composition – a point that attracts the eye and draws the viewer's attention to the work. It should be the centre of interest. Placing the focal point slightly off centre at the intersections of the rule of thirds is seen as the most logical and exciting solution.

A focal point can be created by placing contrasts next to each other in one area, for example, tone (light/dark), colour (complementary colours), shape (round/angular), size (large/small) etc...

The Creative Process | 19

 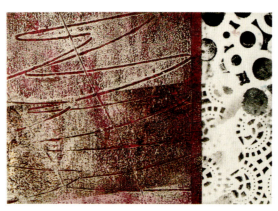

Symmetrical – solemn and static.   Asymmetrical – dynamic, energized.

 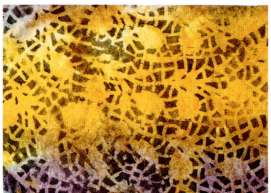

Radial – focusing.   Overall – balanced chaos.

Balance

It is important to achieve balance within a composition (the placing of visual elements), as this affects the way a work is perceived. There are four types of balance used in composition:

- *Symmetrical* – elements on two sides of a central line are mirror images of each other. This repetition leads to a formal or static composition.
- *Asymmetrical* – there is no mirror image in asymmetrical balance, instead it is achieved by using contrasts: one large shape can be balanced by a collection of smaller shapes or a big area of shadow can be balanced with a small area of light. This adds tension and a dynamic quality to the composition.
- *Radial* – elements radiate from a common centre, just as in a stained-glass rose window or an open-faced flower. In this case the focal point is always at the centre.
- *Crystallographic, mosaic or overall balance* – created when elements of equal weight is placed in one area. A balanced chaos is created without a focal point.

Size contrast – large shapes placed against small shapes.

Directional contrast – a way of creating tension and movement in a composition.

Shape contrast – adds variation to the composition.

Light/dark contrast – adds drama to the work.

Quantity contrast – a small area of colour placed in a larger field of another colour.

Colour contrast – a bright, saturated colour set against a duller unsaturated colour.

Contrasts in composition

Contrast involves the juxtaposition of opposing elements in a work. It can be used not only to emphasize the focal point or highlight an area, but also to set the mood in a composition. There are more principles to explore such as pattern, movement and unity. To reinforce your understanding of composition, look at the work of different artists and analyse which sort of compositions they use. For example, symmetrical balance can be found in the work of David Hockney: his compositions are often static. Pollock's work is an example of overall balance in which a focal point is absent. Degas often used asymmetrical balance, where most activity and weigh is placed in one area, leaving more empty space on the opposite side of the work.

Composition exercise

In practice

Always carry your camera or mobile phone with you so that you can capture interesting details and scenes, which can be used as inspiration for you work.

Activate the rule-of-thirds grid on your screen and practise making photographic compositions, ensuring the most important object or detail in your shot lies on or near the grid lines or at the intersections. With time this will become second nature and will save you time having to crop your photos when you need to use them.

In the studio

When you have chosen a theme, analyse the colours you associate with this theme and decide on the colour palette you are going to work with. Build up a collection of magazine clippings in these colours, so that you have a good selection of papers at hand for making collages. You could also create a more personal collection of decorative papers by painting, stamping and screen printing a variety of types of paper, using different media such as acrylic and textile and puff paint, transfer glue and foils etc.

Using these papers, make several collages exploring 'balance' in composition. Analyse the results; are there one or more types of composition that are most suited to the character of your theme?

Consider how you can make these compositions more complex by adding a focal point and creating contrasts. Which mood do you associate with your theme? Does it command strong contrasts for a dramatic effect or subtle contrasts for a softer, atmospheric effect?

When you have produced a series of small paper compositions, choose one to translate into fabric. Decisions now have to be made about the way you will construct the composition (e.g. piecing, appliqué, fusing) and which fabrics you will use. Does texture play a role in your theme, and if so how will you interpret this? Will you rely on textured fabrics, or add hand or machine stitching?

Colour

It's impossible to imagine a world without colour.

In 1666 Isaac Newton discovered that a beam of sunlight can be separated into the following colours visible to the human eye: red, orange, yellow, green, blue, indigo and violet. When light falls on an object, part of it is absorbed and part of it is reflected. So when we see an object as 'red', this colour is reflected and enters our eyes, which then send a signal to the brain to tell us that we see a red colour. A black object absorbs all colours; a white object reflects all colours. We can see that the white light contains many colours by looking at a prism dispersing light, a soap bubble, oil on the street, a CD etc.

For centuries studies have been done on colour, from Leonardo da Vinci, Isaac Newton, Johann Wolfgang von Goethe, Ewald Hering, Michel Eugène Chevreul, Albert Munsell and Wilhelm Ostwald to Johannes Itten. Itten's book *The Elements of Color* is often used in education as well as by artists. Most colour theories, such as those of Johannes Itten, are based on the primary colours red, yellow and blue. These are the colours that cannot be obtained through mixing. Some colour theories also include green as a primary colour.

- The primary colours for painting and printing are lemon yellow, magenta and cyan.
- The primary colours are the most vibrant.
- The secondary colours are obtained by mixing two primary colours:

    yellow and blue = green
    red and blue = purple
    yellow and red = orange

Colours that are positioned opposite each other on the colour wheel are called complementary; mixtures of a primary and a secondary colour are tertiary colours. Shown right are six colours from the colour wheel: red, yellow and blue, and the secondary colours orange, green and purple.

Colour contrasts

In his book *The Elements of Colour* Johannes Itten studies seven colour contrasts:

1. contrast of hue
2. light and dark contrast
3. cold and warm contrast
4. complementary contrast
5. simultaneous contrast
6. contrast of saturation
7. contrast of extension

Contrast of hue – here the primary colours are placed next to each other.

Light and dark contrast – black and white are the two extremes.

Cold and warm contrast –The yellow/orange/red segments form the warm part; the green/blue/purple segments form the cool part.

Complementary contrast – red/green.

Complementary contrast – blue/orange.

Complementary contrast – purple/yellow.

Contrast of saturation – the colours can be bright or muted (mixed).

Contrast of extension – a lot as opposed to a little.

The colours that are opposites on the colour wheel are called complementary and they invigorate each other. Colours that are next to each other, like blue and green, harmonize.

Simultaneous contrast is when we look at a certain colour, and our eyes expect to see its complementary as well, even if it is not there. (Test: First look at a pure colour, then look at a neutral grey surface. This surface appears to take on the hue of the complementary colour. This phenomenon cannot be captured in a photo.)

Colour contrasts in textiles

Contrast of hue.

Light/dark contrast.

Warm/cold contrast.

Complementary contrast.

Saturation contrast.

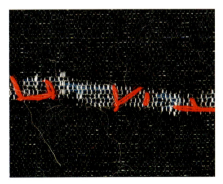
Contrast of extension.

Colours and their meanings

Several studies have been done into people's preferences for certain colours, which are found to be both culture and location bound.

In the Western world blue proves to be the most popular colour, followed by red, although the percentages given by different studies vary.

Some studies have been made that attribute different meanings and associations that are ascribed to various colours:

- *Blue:* expanse, colour of loyalty, coldness and coolness, stillness, the divine, cool colour, seems to recede.
- *Red:* dynamic, fire, love, passion, alarm, advertising, warm colour, comes to the fore.
- *Green:* soothing, fresh, nature, poison, symbolic colour for life, spring, hope.
- *Yellow:* sun, happiness, light, advertisement, signal colour.
- *Purple:* violets, wealth, ecclesiastical colour.
- *Brown:* earth, pettiness, jovial, autumn.
- *White:* purity, clean, fresh, mourning, bridal wear.
- *Black:* mourning, death, hatred, colour of bad luck, colour of fashion, elegance.

In practice

It is important to observe colours intensively under different circumstances. For example, light (daylight or artificial light) affects our perception.

When you dye your own fabrics, you will notice that the same colour dye on different fabrics will yield different results. The texture of the fabric as well as the thread count and weave (satin or twill) play an important role in the outcome.

A colour never stands on its own: it will always be affected by the surrounding colours. In the example opposite a piece of the same colour fabric is shown against different backgrounds.

Looking consciously

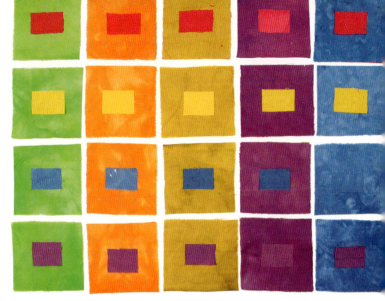

Above: Colour influences on dyed cotton. Notice how the small samples look different on each background colour.

The most important thing of all is to develop an eye for colour. Make it a habit to look around you and record what you see. Where do you mostly see primary colours or secondary colours etc.? Which colours are often used in public spaces, and why do you think that is?

When you look at your surroundings, you will see many inconspicuous colours. These are the colours that are 'difficult' to name; try to unravel how they are made up. Doing this will make you aware of the nuances.

Look at advertisements and packages. For example, which colours are used to make something look 'expensive'? How is a product shown to be a product of Mother Nature?

Take lots of photos, as remembering a colour can be difficult. Through the viewfinder of your camera you can focus on colour compositions. Take several photos from different positions in order to have different focal points.

Break the rules! Perhaps you do not want a focal point at all or you want to have one in an unusual place. All such observations are important for the development of your work.

Colour exercise

You can choose a colour palette for your design in different ways:
- realistically – reflecting reality;
- symbolically – reflecting its meaning;
- 'favourite' colours;
- to suit the environment where the work will be displayed.

Imagine that you are given a commission to make a piece for a certain location. For example:
- a meditation centre;
- a children's hospital;
- a flower shop;
- an IT company.

Come up with a colour palette to suit the nature of each place. Take an A4 sheet of heavy paper or card and glue your main colour and two other colours that you would like to apply in smaller quantities onto it.

This exercise is just about colour choice, it is not meant to be a good design.

CHAPTER 2

GRAVEN IMAGES

Previous page: *It's the Stones that Speak #V* (detail) 102 x 95cm (40 x 37½in), Cherilyn Martin.

The name of a loved one engraved on the inside of a ring, a tribal symbol tattooed on a shoulder and scarification are all forms of engraving.

Scarification is practised in Africa and also in Papua New Guinea. The skin is cut so that scarred tissue is created. Scarification is practised today as an alternative to colourful tattooing; scarring creates decorative patterns on and in the skin. This practice can serve as decoration but is principally carried out as a ceremonial custom to mark the passage from youth into adulthood. Traditionally the scarring practice with a sharp instrument has cultural meaning and belongs to tribal traditions. It appears to be an ancient tradition as Egyptian mummies have been found with evidence of scarification.

When we talk about graven images we mean images carved out of stone, wood or metal. These could include a statue of a person or animal, or a relief carving in a wall or on a pole. Carved wooden poles and etchings of gods accompanying Egyptian hieroglyphics can all be classed as graven images.

Gravestones

Since the days of Charlemagne (around 785), by law the dead had to be buried, not cremated, except in times of contagious diseases and war. It was thought that more respect would be paid to the deceased by burying the body as close as possible to the altar, the most sacred place, and large sums were paid by families to have the gravestone of a loved one inside a church.

We decided to work on the themes of 'Gravestones in the Netherlands'. The traces of time and the elements give gravestones a weathered appearance that opens up a range of textural opportunities and provides a means of giving form to the associated concepts of death and decay. Visiting different cemeteries gives an insight into the different styles of remembrance.

Some graves are sober, while others are abundantly decorated. So, how can you begin working with this theme?

One option is to study the image of a gravestone, focus on a particular shape and take that as the basis for your work. This shape can be repeated, mirrored or cut up into an abstract interpretation.The texts you read can evoke a memory.

30 | Graven Images

As well as graves, inscriptions, graffiti, or even a line in the sand can also offer inspiration.

This theme can also be extended to cave paintings. There are books available with detailed images that could be the start for a textile work. For example, you could study ancient cave paintings, like those at Lascaux, France, which offer a wealth of line, colour and nuances. Many artists have been inspired by them. It is fascinating to consider that these mysterious paintings were made such a long time ago and yet contain so much energy and verve. Consider how modern wall art compares.

All textured surfaces invite us to feel them with our hands. Making a print of this texture is the next step, as explained overleaf.

Top left: Egyptian hieroglyphics.

Bottom left: Impression on wet sand.

Top right: Gravestone from around 1690.

Bottom right: Inscription dated 1887.

Graven Images | 31

Rubbing

From childhood we all remember rubbing a pencil over a coin placed under a sheet of paper. It was like magic: all of a sudden an image would come to life! However, this technique has much more to offer.

The history of rubbing

It is possible that the first rubbings were made in China. Stone-rubbings, which inspired the invention of printing, have a long history in China, and the medium most used for long inscriptions was stone. From 175 to 183, the seven Confucian classic texts in over 200,000 characters were carved on forty-six poles made of stone, front and back, to establish and preserve standard versions of the texts for students and scholars. It was an early method of making multiple copies.

The works were made by pressing thin sheets of wet paper in the inscriptions cut in stone. When the paper was almost dry, black ink was applied on the surface. The result: the impressions of the carvings are white; the background is black.

Right: Chinese rubbing.

32 | Graven Images

Left: *Time*, 2 x 50 x 100cm (¾ x 19½ x 39in), Els van Baarle. Wax, dye, paint, screenprint.

Below: Gravestone outside Brouwershaven church, with moss growing in the inscriptions.

Els's interpretation

When executing this theme I made use of gravestones in the church of Brouwershaven, which is in the province of Zeeland in the Netherlands. This building dates back to 1325; parts of it have been added later. Originally this was a Catholic church and in the Iconoclastic Fury of 1566 Protestants destroyed Catholic Church imagery and symbols on gravestones were hacked away. Inscriptions, however, were spared.

Graven Images | 33

Left: Gravestone rubbing with stitching, detail, 90 x 220cm (35 x 86½in) Silk.

The people themselves have long been forgotten; just their names still exist.

> 'Only through writing
> the dead will remain in the
> memory of the living
> and can those who are far apart
> converse as if they were together.'
> DIODORUS SICULUS

The gravestones in this church have texts in high relief as well as low relief. Els was given permission to take prints of these texts: she put fabric over the stones and made rubbings of both the relief and engraved texts to produce either a positive or a negative image.

Working method

In order to get a good print the fabric needs to be tightly woven. Silk gives a good result, as does thin cotton. Fabric was taped to the stone, pulling it as taut as possible. The paint used for this project was opaque Pébéo Setacolor. A brayer was sparingly covered with paint and then rolled over the fabric. The result is an angular image with fragments of paint. Using different paints and tools will give a different effect.

34 | Graven Images

Further work on this project is possible: you could paint the background, e.g. with Procion dye or textile paint; you could add embroidery to the painted background or make an appliqué or you could partially cover the rubbing with wax before applying paint. By repeating this process depth can be achieved.

Decide which techniques are the most important for you. Overworking might cause the subject of the print to become unrecognisable. If this is not your intention you must carefully consider every step. After making the rubbing, I proceed as follows:

- The paint is set by ironing. Once ironed, parts of the fabric are covered with wax, using a brush or tjanting tool.
- The next step is to apply Procion dye. Multiple layers of wax and dye result in depth and mystery, which suit the subject well.
- Finally the wax is removed. (Depending on the type of wax, this can be done either by boiling, ironing or dry-cleaning.) The work is highlighted with hand embroidery.
A number of works were made from several gravestones. I intentionally chose light shades of colour. The emphasis is on the date of death (e.g. 1677) or the age of the deceased. I accentuated these by applying seed stitches.

Below: *Hieronder Rust #1*, 140 x 120cm (55 x 47in), Els van Baarle. Rubbing and stitching on silk.

Cherilyn's interpretation

Brass rubbing has been a popular hobby for many decades. There is a rich legacy of commemorative brasses in churches and these give easy access to social and cultural history.

The laying of incised slabs and brass plates has been commonplace in Europe since medieval times. They were used to cover the tombs of those buried in churches and served as memorials or monuments to the deceased. The earliest incised slabs we know of date from the eighth to the tenth centuries and feature simple crosses or inscriptions, most commonly on sandstone and limestone.

From the late eleventh century engraving became more elaborate, featuring depictions of the deceased. Gradually slabs were enriched with metal details: hands and faces for example were depicted in metal, which was inlaid into the stone. This led to the development of brasses, which

Above: Examples of incised floor slabs found in 14th-century English Parish Churches.

featured the entire figure. The making of increasingly elaborate brasses continued until their decline in the late seventeenth century.

The production of brass plates was revived again during the Victorian era, when richly ornate monuments became fashionable.

There are many surviving brasses in the UK. During the medieval and early modern periods many brasses were laid in Continental European countries, and most of the surviving ones are to be found in Germany and Poland, with rather fewer in Belgium and France.

These brasses and slabs serve as a testament of social and cultural history, reflecting general trends in the art of their period and a documentation of prominent figures in European history.

Modern brass memorial plaques

The work of the German artist Gunter Demnig (b.1947, Berlin) shows how the use of brass memorial plaques continues to be relevant. With the 'Stolpersteine' project ('Stumbling blocks') Demnig lays memorial stones in pavements outside of the homes of people who were deported by the Nazis, who were killed or driven to suicide. Other groups besides Jews who are commemorated are Jehovah's Witnesses, Sinti and Roma gypsies, political prisoners, homosexuals and disabled people. Demnig calls these stones stumbling blocks, because you stumble across them as you walk through a neighbourhood where those who are commemorated once lived.

The first stone was laid in Cologne in 1992, outside of the city hall, in commemoration of the fiftieth anniversary of the deportation order of thousands of Roma and Sinti gypsies. The first sentence of the order is engraved in the stone.

This was followed in 1995 by the first 'Stolpersteine', which Demnig laid without permission from the authorities in Cologne. Each block (10 x 10cm/4 x 4in) is incised with the name, date of birth and deportation, and finally with the date and place of death of the person. Originally Demnig made and laid the blocks himself, but due to the popularity of the project he had to enlist help from a fellow artist. Demnig however always lays the first block himself when working on a new commission, and only when additional blocks are commissioned to an old site, others may lay them. By the end of 2015 more than 56,000 blocks had been laid throughout Europe.

Above: Examples of Gunter Demnig's *Stolpersteine* in Berlin.

Right: *Homage to Gunter Demnig #1*, made in response to Demnig's *Stolpersteinen*, 97 x 68cm (38 x 26½in), Cherilyn Martin. Appliqué, quilting, acrylic paint, oil paint stick, paper and inkjet photocopy on organza.

Right: *It's the Stones that Speak #V*, 102 x 95cm (40 x 37½in), Cherilyn Martin.

Cemeteries

Cemeteries are places of contemplation, filled with a fascinating array of headstones and graves weathered by time and the elements: inscriptions that have faded with time, graves which have disintegrated and stone slabs which are gradually reclaimed by Nature. These are all elements that serve as inspiration and which challenge me to consider the form my work will take.

Tearing sections of fabric or paper and overlapping panels to create the suggestion of fragmented or cracked surfaces has become a feature of my work. Exploring texture through surface manipulation and the use of stitch is a main priority.

It's the Stones that Speak #V was made in response to this theme. This work is made from layered paper, which has undergone several treatments. Firstly the paper layers were laminated (glued together) and then painted with Procion MX dye. The central panel features rubbed surfaces, text painted in by hand and subsequently painted with diluted gesso to create a weathered effect.

Other panels have been intensively stitched by hand and machine, after which another layer of gesso was added. Leaves made with machine embroidery on water soluble film have been applied to the surface, together with twigs, which have been wrapped with thread.

40 | Graven Images

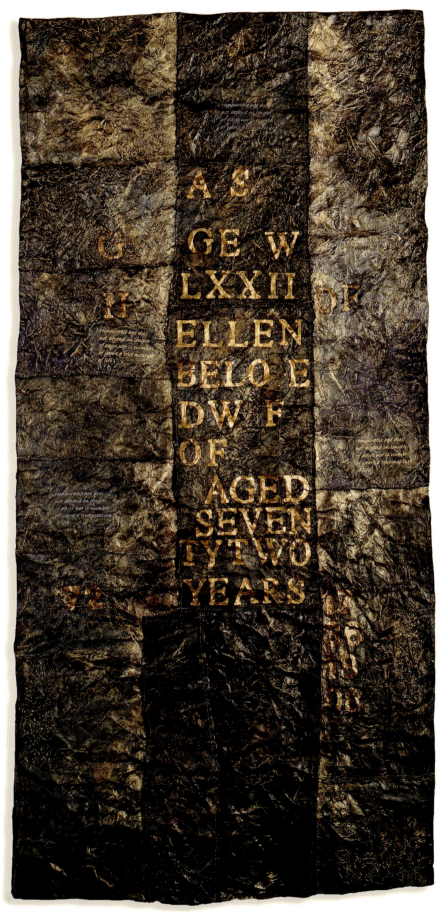

Top: Headstone to a family grave. Rubbings were made of the headstone and translated into a paper quilt construction.

Above: Wax-crayon rubbing.

Right: *Graven Images #6*, 165 x 95cm (65 x 37½in), Cherilyn Martin. This piece was made in response to details on the headstone of a family grave.

Graven Images | 41

Right: Trapunto and machine embroidery on silk, covered with Tissuetex and surface rubbed with wax crayon to enhance texture.

Suggestions for interpretation

Take a series of photos in a graveyard near to where you live. Look at the way the gravestones have become worn by time and how Nature has had an impact on the stones. How could you interpret this information in your work? Are you interested more in the surfaces or the shapes of the stones? Think about repetition and the way depth is created as you look at the gravestones in the distance. Make rubbings of the inscriptions you find interesting. The weathered surfaces of stones reveal countless marks, scratches and details, which can be translated into stitch. Colour, lines and dots can be reproduced by combining embroidery and decorative threads and by stitching creatively. Depth can be achieved by layering stitches, using darker tones underneath and working with lighter tones on the surface. Texture can be created by using 'texture' stitches (French knots, bullion stitch, couching etc.) in combination with thick threads.

To re-create the high relief of sculpted images found on tombstones, the trapunto technique can be used; shapes are stitched through two layers of fabric, which are then padded from the back of the work by hand, to create raised areas on the surface. Further embroidery can be added for extra texture.

Above: Transfer paint/crayons and hand embroidery on polyester batting, Cherilyn Martin.

Variations on the rubbing technique

It is not always possible to make rubbings in situ. When working in the studio an interesting alternative is to use commercially produced rubbing plates, which are readily available.

Transfer paint and transfer crayons are used in the following experiment. Choose a suitable synthetic fabric (woven or non-woven) as a base. Non-wovens such as Evolon, Lutradur or even polyester batting can be used.

Method

- Paint copy paper with transfer paint and allow the paper to dry.
- Place painted side down onto synthetic fabric and iron from the back. The colour transfers onto the fabric.
- Using transfer crayons, take a rubbing from a rubbing plate of your choice.
- The rubbing can then be ironed face down onto the coloured synthetic fabric.
- Ironing heat-fixes the colour in the fibres of the fabric.
- To add extra texture and details, the surface can then be embroidered by hand.

Of course you can choose your own colour palette when working with this theme; the same technique using another colour palette gives a totally different effect.

CHAPTER 3

WALLS

Previous page:
Walls #8, 22 x 22cm (8½ x 8½in), Cherilyn Martin. Handmade paper, machine pieced, screen-printed with textile paint, puff paint, foils and foil glue.

Protection, defence, division, barriers, enclosures and symbols are some of the powerful words associated with the construction of walls, some of which have quite negative connotations – there are many walls still being erected as an attempt to contain political and cultural diversity, and to limit the movement of people.

More positively, walls offer shelter and contain doors and gateways, which allow us to cross the threshold from one reality to the next.

Walls are inspirational, and their impact profound. Strolling through a city armed with a camera is the best way to capture both overall impressions and finer details. Observation and learning to look are the first steps on our creative journey. It is essential at first to be receptive and absorb the phenomena encountered; at a later stage you can make more informed personal choices about how best to proceed with the processing of this information.

Cherilyn's interpretation

Walls have been a recurring theme in my work over the years. Through my travels I have had the opportunity to collect interesting visual information of a variety of architectural styles which has informed much of my work. Spending long periods in Greece and Italy has given me the opportunity to study Greek and Roman architecture first hand. Discovering unexpected details among the ruins can be inspirational.

46 | Walls

Walls are parameters which impact on our daily lives. Our houses, places of work and study are all defined by walls and buildings that quite often create beautiful and inspirational urban landscapes. The architectural hodgepodge that surrounds us, and the juxtaposition of different scales is fascinating. Doors and windows are integral parts of buildings. As you study them, consider their relationship with the structure: Are they a dominant feature, as seen in modern high-rise buildings, where enormous walls are clad with glass panels – imposing, maybe clinical and impersonal? Or are they the windows and doors of old buildings, smaller in scale, more intimate and decorative? The character of these buildings is defined by weathered stonework showing the effects of time passing.

Below: *Secrets of Caestert #1*, detail, 109 x 109cm (43 x 43in), Cherilyn Martin. Machine-pieced paper, surface treated with diverse media.

Above: Sampler for *Walls #4*, 100 x 100cm (39 x 39in), Cherilyn Martin. Collaged paper and fabric, machine-quilted and added machine embroidery.

Walls as inspiration

Demolition sites are intriguing and offer a wealth of ideas. Walls are torn down, exposing the core of the building, giving an insight into the lives of previous inhabitants. Peeling wallpaper, the odd picture still hanging on a wall, broken windows, a torn curtain blowing in the wind, all become part of a narrative.

As you photograph, sketch and study them you become aware of the superimposition of walls within the structure, of the visual depth created by this physical layering. The fragmented silhouettes of buildings and shapes of broken walls can become the starting point for new work. Explore the possibility of creating work that reflects these shapes – odd shapes that challenge the restrictions of the rectangle or square.

Your photographs and sketches are a great starting point for making mixed-media collages, which in turn can become designs for a piece of work.

- Collect textured fabrics and papers and make a series of collages based on your photos. Look at the contrast of soft torn edges next to hard cut edges.
- Consider how to re-create the effect of peeling. Pieces of heat-manipulated organza can be used as overlays for example.
- Use Bondaweb or Spunfab to fuse layers of thread and organza, then stich into the surface to add texture.
- The painterly effect of fragmented coloured surfaces can be achieved by mono printing with textile paint on fabric. The colours can be worked into with hand stitching and puff paint applied for textural effects.

Right: *Walls #4*, Cherilyn Martin. Batik silk (Els van Baarle), mixed fabrics and paper, machine quilting and embroidery.

Structure

Methods of construction and materials used in wall building vary enormously. This provides us with a wealth of information to use as the starting point for a project. Gathering this information is paramount; again photograph all types of wall construction you encounter on your outings. In the British and Irish countryside dry-stone walling is common, and provides us with beuatiful organic structures. Walls can be made from different kinds of natural stone, which have different colourings and characteristics, such as granite, sandstone and slate. More common is the use of fabricated fired clay bricks primarily used in the construction of small buildings. In larger high-rise buildings use is made of concrete and steel; in these cases repetition of shape is interesting.

Above: *Walls #1*, detail, 100 x 100cm (39 x 39in), Cherilyn Martin. Strip piecing and machine quilting.

Interpretations in fabric and paper

Above right:
Sampler, Cherilyn Martin. Tyvek machine-stitched onto a base fabric and painted with puff paint. Painted with textile paint and heated with heat gun. Transfer foil-ironed onto surface.

Above left:
Sampler, Cherilyn Martin. Machine embroidery painted with puff paint and textile paint, heated with heat gun and stitched into with metallic thread.

Look closely at the photos you have collected of wall structures and analyse the forms that occur in the images. Make a collection of textured fabrics you could use for sampling, in the same colour palette as the walls. Collect any other fabrics you may need, such as batting and support fabrics. Make a list of techniques you could use to interpret wall structures.

Here are some suggestions:

- Prepare a quilt sandwich and collage and pin small pieces of various fabrics to the top layer. Tack layers securely and machine quilt using the normal quilting foot. To achieve different effects, experiment with the density of quilting.

- Experiment with strip piecing (see *Walls #1*, opposite). Sew pieces of fabric together into long strips. Cut the strips to the same length and sew them together to make a pieced fabric. The strips can be placed horizontally, vertically or diagonally in a design. The pieced fabric can then be quilted to add relief and stability.

- Different textures can be explored by combining paper and fabric, using the two construction methods mentioned above. When using paper in a sewing project it is advisable to reinforce it with iron-on cotton or Vilene as a backing, so that it does not disintegrate with machine stitching.

- Tear pieces of textured paper to resemble the shapes of stones in your photos. Iron on a

Walls | 51

stabiliser, as mentioned above. Sew pieces together by hand or machine to re-create a wall structure. The pieced construction can then be painted if desired and extra details added.

- Fuse small pieces of fabric onto a base fabric with Bondaweb to resemble patterns of stonework. Work into the fabric with machine embroidery to give the impression of textures created by algae on stone.
- Try reworking an old quilted sample you may have. Colour with Procion dye or with acrylic paint, so that the structure of the quilting becomes more evident and patterns in the fabric disappear. Highlight the raised surface by rubbing with a metallic paint stick; the surface takes on a stone/wall-like appearance.

Graffiti

It is not just the stone, shape and texture of a wall that is worth studying. In many places we can see that walls have been written on or spray-painted. Graffiti is the generic term for imagery and texts on walls in public places and is derived from the Italian word *graffiare*, which means to scratch.

Writing on walls has a long history. Around 40,000 BCE cave dwellers made cave paintings. We also see examples of graffiti in antiquity. The Romans wrote political slogans and announcements for gladiator games on the walls. Excavations at Pompeii have revealed some interesting examples, and for centuries it has been customary for city-dwellers to daub on walls.

Throughout history conquerors have left their mark. In Rome, inscriptions made by Vikings, have been found. Crusaders carved crosses in the Church of the Holy Sepulchre in Jerusalem. It has always been important for people to leave their mark or name on surfaces.

Graffiti, as we know it today, has its origins in the 1940s. During the Second World War it was fashionable among American soldiers to leave the words 'Kilroy was here' on walls, tanks or aeroplanes. This would confuse the enemy troops, who wondered what these three words meant.

The origin of this text is not very clear. A possible explanation could be the following account: James J. Kilroy was an inspector at a shipyard where battleships were built. Inspected parts were marked with the words 'Kilroy was here' as a sign of approval.

After the war the practice of graffiti grew. In the 1960s young people in American cities would write pseudonyms on walls and trains, using markers or spray-paint. Such a stylised signature or symbol by the graffitist is called a 'tag' or 'scribble'. A competing graffitist would scratch over it with his own signature or symbol. The speed of writing was more important than a beautiful design.

From America, this practice of graffiti spread to Europe. The creations varied from being plain vandalism to a colourful art form. These days there are well-established graffiti artists who make extremely complicated wall paintings that are greatly appreciated.

Every country and/or city has its own graffiti policy and rules for which forms of graffiti are allowed. Some artists use stencils made out of cardboard or other material. The stencil is used with spray paint or roll-on paint, and can be used several times. You can even buy books with readymade stencils, for you to use on different backgrounds like paper, fabric or walls.

Above (top row): Graffiti in Melbourne, Australia.

Above: (bottom row, left) Graffiti in Doel, Belgium. The Council of Antwerp decided to expand their harbour and the village had to disperse. The houses remained, all covered with graffiti. It has become a ghost town.

Above (bottom row, right): Wall in Fort Rammekens, the Netherlands.

Walls | 53

Graffiti as source of inspiration

Examples of graffiti can be found everywhere. As with all themes, begin by studying them carefully. It is worthwhile taking photos from different angles. There is no need for a painting to be 'beautiful' for it to be suitable as the starting point for your work. Consider the following:

- Can you look beyond the letters and see the lines and planes?
- Does the direction of the lines express dynamics?
- Is there contrast in form or colour?
- Do the planes have contour lines? What colour are they?
- Does the texture of the wall play an important role?
- Looking at your photos on the computer, is there any picture that needs to be cropped or enlarged? This could become a powerful design.

Make your own 'tag'

Search for examples of 'tags' on buildings or trains. They will not be hard to find, but look for variations. Notice that many 'tags' are in black. Now use your own initials to make a design for a textile work. Which techniques could you apply? Make a list of techniques and materials, or make a mind map.

Right: Graffiti in Melbourne, Australia, detail. This pattern may remind you of embroidery stitches, or can be used as an inspiration for mark-making. It is a very lively pattern, because of the spontaneous way the background is covered. Look at the different directions of the paint, there is movement and this makes the design interesting.

54 | Walls

Here are some suggestions:
- appliqué
- embroidery
- quilting
- weaving
- stencilling
- screen-printing
- painting
- working with wax and tjanting tool or brush
- collage
- encaustic collage

Try the following exercises on a sheet of white watercolour paper:
- Using a brush and Indian ink, start making quick, spontaneous drawings. Fill your brush with so much ink that it drips on your paper. Hold the paper upright in order for the drops to leave a trace.
- Take black acrylic paint and a bristle brush. Apply a very small amount of paint to the brush and move it quickly over the paper in order to leave visible brush marks.
- Tape two markers together, one thick and one thin. When you draw, this double pen will leave two different lines. You can vary these lines by holding the pen at an angle.
- Repeat with ink, using two sticks taped together.
- Stretch a piece of fabric over a framework and place this in a vertical position. Now, paint symbols or letters on it. The effect will depend on the consistency of the paint. Thickened paint will give a different result than dye.
- Explore as many possibilities as you can!

Look how the outlines of the letters are made; some will have a black line, others a light colour around the edges. Some have two colours, or have a pattern that makes a shadow. Look at the way depth is suggested.

These 'drawings' will be usable designs, e.g. for embroidery.

We construct and keep constructing, yet intuition is still a good thing.
Paul Klee

Top and centre: *Tags* in progress, Cherilyn Martin. Rust techniques and embroidery.

Above: *Tags*, Els van Baarle. Silkscreen with mixed media.

Walls | 55

Top: Wall in China. Look at the numbers and notice how the paint has dripped.

Left: *Chinese Memory #4*, 35 x 85cm (13¾ x 33½in), Els van Baarle. Paper, wax, fabric.

Above: Dye, paint, stencil and silkscreen on cotton. 27 x 30cm (10½ x 12in), Els van Baarle.

Top right: *Nothing is the Same #1*, detail, Els van Baarle.

Far right: *Graffiti #V1'*, 90 x 240cm (35½ x 94½in), Els van Baarle. Wax, dye, discharge, silkscreen on velvet.

Right centre: Wax, dye, silkscreen on cotton, 60 x 50cm (23½ x 19½in), Els van Baarle.

Right: Wax, dye, silkscreen, stitch on silk (detail), 40 x 145cm (15¾ x 57in), Els van Baarle.

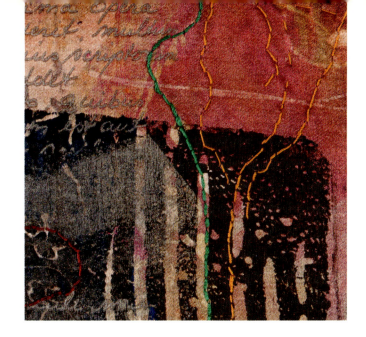

CHAPTER 4
POMPEII

A little history

During the warm month of August CE 79, earth tremors were felt in the Italian region of Campania, around Mount Vesuvius. The local population was used to these tremors, as they occurred frequently.

In the year CE 62, a large earthquake had caused severe damage to the cities around the volcano. The earth tremors of 24 August CE 79 would have made people afraid that something similar might happen again; an impending eruption of the volcano would not have occurred to them.

As usual, the inhabitants of Pompeii began their daily routine early in the morning; farmers went to their fields and vineyards, which stretched out almost as far as the volcano. Slaves began their domestic work; bakers made bread and shopkeepers displayed their wares. People were not prepared for the impending disaster.

Mount Vesuvius erupted totally unexpectedly; there had been no warning signs of growing activity. It was a violent explosion – a column of lava shot up high into the air, followed by grit, rocks and gases. In just two days the entire area was buried under a layer of volcanic material, as thick as 5m (16ft) in places. The towns of Pompeii, Herculaneum, Oplontis, Stabiae and Boscoreale had disappeared from view.

Previous page: *Oplontis #III* (detail), Els van Baarle.

Above: On these walls various subjects such as birds, fish, fruit and mythological scenes were painted with great skill.

The town of Pompeii

Above right: Naturalistic frescoes were also found on the walls of shops, hostels and street altars.

Pompeii, a town of around 20,000 inhabitants, was a lively place. The population was made up of slaves, freemen, the middle classes and the wealthy. There were shops, temples, inns and public baths, as well as an amphitheatre and a gladiator arena. Along the coast were the villas of the Roman aristocracy.

The consequences of the severe earthquake of CE 62 were still visible, and rebuilding had not yet been finished when ash and rocks from the eruption of Mount Vesuvius buried the town. This became evident during excavations, when partly rebuilt walls, renovated mosaics, building materials and tools emerged from underneath the layer of volcanic debris.

The houses of the wealthy inhabitants of Pompeii were very impressive. Inside and outside there were bronze statues and marble benches. They had magnificent mosaic floors, made up of miniscule pieces of glass in a wealth of colours. The walls of their homes were painted with frescoes. Illusion was important; the rooms seemed to go on endlessly, stretching out into rolling landscapes or rock formations under blue skies. The walls were divided into large planes, often in black, red and yellow.

Left: *Pompeii ... the People*, 140 x 180cm (55 x 71in), Els van Baarle. Detail of work based on the cast of one of the victims. Wax, batik, dyed and discharged, with screen-print and stitch on cotton velvet.

The inhabitants

A large number of Pompeii's inhabitants managed to flee. In the town the bodies of around 2,000 perished people were found. They were lying in basements or other sheltered places, where they probably thought they would be safe. Some people tried to reach the city gates, carrying with them art objects and purses containing jewellery and coins. The clouds of gases and lava surprised them in their flight. Their bodies were covered with moist ash, which formed a solid layer; escape was impossible. The whole area remained untouched for centuries.

Excavations

In the mid-18th century the first intentional excavations were undertaken and many objects that were found at the different sites can now be seen in the Archaeological Museum in Naples.

Around 1870 Giuseppe Fiorelli, the head of excavations, discovered that the hollows created by the bodies underneath the petrified layer of ash could be filled with plaster. Accurate casts were thus made of the bodies, sometimes even with details of clothing. Some of the casts of victims are in very poignant poses, such as mothers protectively bending over their children. We can imagine the horrific fate that befell them. They are images that still move us today.

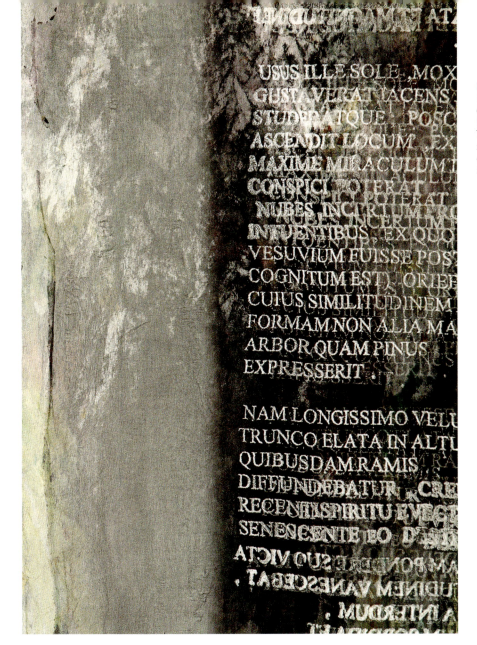

Left: *Text – Plinius*, 3 x 70 x 240cm (1 x 27½ x 94½in), Els van Baarle. Three layers of silk organza, dye, discharge, silkscreen.

Pliny the Younger

There is an eyewitness account of the disaster. At the time of the eruption Pliny (Plinius) the Younger (literary figure and magistrate) was staying on the coast at Miseno. From there he witnessed the explosion of Mount Vesuvius. In two long letters to his friend Tacitus he describes the events of 24 and 25 August. Although historians are not convinced that these epistles are entirely genuine.

His uncle, Pliny the Elder – commander-in-chief of the fleet – departed from Miseno for the coast of Pompeii with a number of ships, to see whether he could be of assistance. He left late in the afternoon on 24 August, but was not able to land at Stabiae until 25 August. It is believed that Pliny the Elder suffocated on the beach.

Pompeii | 63

Villa Poppaea, Oplontis

Above: Wall with fresco in Villa Poppaea.

Oplontis is a remarkable location. Here two large villas were excavated, of which the Villa Poppaea is the most important.

Poppaea was the second wife of Emperor Nero. She was the owner of a luxurious villa, which was probably being renovated at the time of the eruption. Building materials were found in the rooms and it is likely that only servants were present at the time. The complex contains gardens, a pool, a large reception hall and more than twenty other rooms. The villa is particularly famous for its rich, well-preserved wall paintings. Here, too, there is the illusion that the space of the room is indefinite.

Pompeii and its surroundings as a theme

This theme offers a wide range of possibilities and choices will have to be made. Make a mind map or a list of the aspects that speak to you, such as:

- architecture
- lifestyle of the population
- objects excavated
- casts of the bodies
- clothing
- writing
- frescoes
- mosaics
- gods and myths
- colour

Inspiration

It is important to read extensively about your subject, even when you think something only indirectly relates to it. This can deepen your work. Working with a theme encourages you to take things further. For instance, challenge yourself to make ten works on the same subject; this will stimulate your creativity. They do not have to be masterpieces, but force yourself not to give up.

Right: Photographs taken in Oplontis, used for inspiration.

Els's interpretation

The theme of Pompeii and its surroundings has been an ongoing project for us both. As far back as the mid-1990s Cherilyn and I exhibited together at the renowned Gallery Smend in Cologne; the title of this exhibition was 'Oplontis'.

For a long time my knowledge of the excavations at Pompeii came from books, which often show the same images in those familiar bright colours. It was not until I visited the excavation site myself, that I was introduced to a completely different colour palette. I was surprised to see the more subdued hues, which have become the basis for my new work.

Far left: Wall in Villa Poppaea in Oplontis.

Left and right: *Oplontis #III* (details), Els van Baarle.

Below: *Oplontis #III*, 15 x 280cm (6 x 110in), Els van Baarle.

Pompeii | 67

Working method for Oplontis #III

- Both sides of heavy white cotton were covered with hot wax, a 50/50 mixture of beeswax and paraffin. I used a wide, flat hog brush to apply the wax.
- The fabric was then placed in the freezer for a little while. The low temperature makes the wax nice and hard and the paraffin in the mixture causes the wax to crackle; this creates the effect of a weathered wall. Using a blunt needle I scratched marks and letters in the hardened wax. The fabric was then put into a black Procion MX dye bath. After an hour it was rinsed and dried.
- If you try this process yourself, you will notice that in order to achieve the desired effect, it is sometimes necessary to repeat the different steps.
- When your work is finished the excess wax needs to be removed by ironing the fabric between sheets of paper.

Safety

- Always follow the supplier's instructions.
- Use a mask and gloves when handling dyes.
- Be aware of fumes; some materials can only be used with proper ventilation.
- Be careful with hot wax; use a safe wax pot, with a proper working thermostat.
- Always start working at the lowest temperature. The wax is hot enough if it penetrates the fabric.
- In case of fumes, cool the wax down by adding new wax.
- Always keep a lid next to the pot.

Left: Walls decorated with frescoes featuring scenes from nature, photographed in Oplontis.

Cherilyn's interpretation

Thorough research into a chosen theme can offer a wealth of new ideas that can be used to inform our work. While working on the theme of Pompeii and Oplontis, I became aware of the Pompeiians' love of horticulture and of the importance that gardens played in Roman life. Nearly all houses had some type of garden. An 'ordinary' citizen would have had a small area at the back of his house in which vegetables and herbs were grown, known as a 'hortus'.

Wealthy people constructed lavish walled gardens, which were used as an extension to their living quarters. As a rule rooms were arranged around an interior garden, which often had a water feature such as a fountain or a pool. Such a garden (called an atrium) offered respite from the heat and was used as an outdoor dining area or for entertaining. It would be elaborately planted with trees, flowering plants and shrubs and, of course herbs and fruit. The surrounding walls were often painted with frescoes, echoing the Roman love of nature. These frescoes created an illusion of depth in the garden and featured fountains with birds and other animals. The Romans also 'brought the outside in', by painting the walls of the atrium with landscapes and scenes from nature.

These frescoes were painted with a solution of pigments mixed with lime and soap mix. Beeswax was also added. When dry, the surface was burnished with a polishing stone and buffed with a cloth. This is an early example of the use of encaustic in wall painting.

 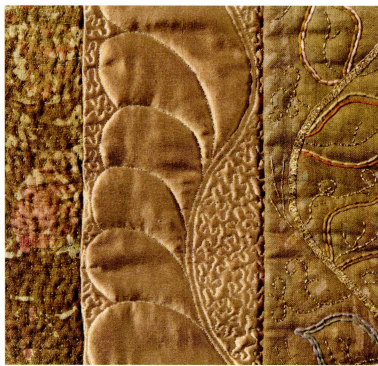

Being inspired by excavations

Above left: Frescoes featuring decorative panels.

Above right: *Giardino Antico #2*, detail, 140 x 145cm (55 x 57in), Cherilyn Martin. Hand embroidery and free-motion machine quilting on batik silk and linen.

Right: *Parete #5*, 55 x 45cm (21½ x 17½in), Cherilyn Martin. Batik silk (Els van Baarle), space-dyed scrim, hand and machine quilting, hand embroidery.

While researching your subject you can ask yourself which elements appeal to you the most and which you want to interpret in your work. For example, not only is colour important in Roman garden frescoes, but also the details of plants, flowers and animals. Taking a closer look you can see the effects of the passing of time on these surfaces. Peeling paint, fragmented images and the exposure of the bare stone foundations are fascinating details for further investigation.

The *Parete* series was made in response to the intense colour of Pompeiian frescoes. The batik marks in the border hint at plant forms depicted on walls. *Parete #5* has been intensely embroidered, echoing the textures of ageing surfaces. The top layer of scrim adds mystery to the piece, hinting at the layers of time passing.

Interior walls of Pompeiian villas were often painted with panels featuring mythological subjects, still lives and landscapes set in a framework of ornamental architectural elements. This juxtaposition of naturalistic and formal elements was the starting point for a series of works that carry the title *Giardino Antico*.

Above left: Design sheet of architectural details in Pompeii, Cherilyn Martin.

Above right: *Parete #2*, detail, 110 x 110cm (43 x 43in), Cherilyn Martin.

Looking beyond the colourful frescoes of Pompeii, the sculptural elements of Roman architecture are equally fascinating. As Els has noted, when visiting Pompeii one is faced with an imposing monochromatic sea of ruins and endless streets and alleyways. It is a welcome interruption when one comes across parts of frescoes on crumbling walls and eventually a spectacular villa with its colourful frescoes still virtually intact.

Among this grey vastness are many decorative details of Roman architecture, such as a lintel with carvings or inscriptions, broken columns and richly carved capitals featuring organic forms such as acanthus leaves. These are jewels that attract our attention and can serve as inspiration.

Here are some observations that may help you:

- Recording your findings with a camera is the most effective way of gathering information.
- Sketching is invaluable as it forces you to look closer at the subject matter and become more familiar with it. Draw both general impressions and detailed pictures.
- A design sheet can serve as a base from which you can develop ideas for new work.

Right: *Parete #6*, detail, 140 x 120cm (55 x 47in), Cherilyn Martin.

Interpreting motifs in quilt work

- Using a pencil, draw a selected motif by hand onto tracing paper.
  Tack this drawing securely onto a prepared quilt sandwich base.
  Prepare your sewing machine for free-motion sewing (lower the feed dogs and attach a darning foot).
- Begin quilting by pulling the bottom thread to the surface, make a few stitches in the quilt sandwich and cut off the thread ends. You can now quilt without hindrance from loose threads.
- Continue free motion quilting by following the pencil lines without making any stops. Think about the quilting route before sewing begins.
- When sewing is completed, tear the tracing paper carefully away from the quilt sandwich.
- When the motif is completed, consider if the background needs to be filled in with a quilt technique such as meandering or seeding to highlight the relief of the motif.

Parete #6 is made from batik cotton batist (cambric). Block prints using metallic textile paint refer to motifs found in Roman architecture. The work has been further enriched with hand and machine quilting and embroidery, which echoes the heavily decorative Roman interpretation of Classical Greek architecture, as found in the ruins of Pompeii.

The spirit of Pompeii lives on through our creative work.

CHAPTER 5

YESTERDAY IS HISTORY

Above: Design sheet, motifs and patterning taken from the Bayeux tapestry as inspiration for surface design and stitch. Cherilyn Martin.

Everyone has their own memories; as an artist you can strive to visualise your thoughts on memory in your work. Memory as inspiration can cover many areas; not only personal experiences but also historical events. Textiles have always been an important vehicle for recording social history, whether demonstrating social position or for storytelling.

For centuries embroidery has played an important role in both secular and ecclesiastical European textiles, documenting fashions and different periods of artistic development. During the Middle Ages luxurious robes featured graphic illustrations to reflect the wealth and importance of the monarchy and nobility. Sumptuous fabrics were richly decorated with exquisite silk and metallic threads using intricate hand embroidery. Unfortunately, few of these early ornamental garments have survived.

The coveted Bayeux Tapestry (c.1070–7) is an epic embroidery and a unique historical document. Made from a band of linen cloth measuring nearly 70m (230ft) long and 50cm (19½in) in height, it consists of nine panels of varying lengths, which were embroidered individually and then joined together. It depicts events leading up to the Norman conquest of England, culminating in the Battle of Hastings. Its graphic scenes are embroidered with naturally dyed woollen yarns, and Latin texts known as 'tituli' have been added to explain

events and to name important personages. These texts also give clarity to the simplified images.

Early ecclesiastical embroidery was a means of teaching and illustrating religious faith to the illiterate masses. Figures of saints were depicted clearly on vestments worn by the clergy, placed so that they were visible to all. They were sumptuously embroidered and embellished with precious stones.

With 'Opus Anglicanum' (c.12 to 14th centuries) the golden age of English embroidery followed. Work for both liturgical and secular use was produced and designs were lavishly worked in gold, silver and silk threads on luxurious background fabrics such as velvet and linen. Opus Anglicanum is renowned for the use of detail and shading, and expression achieved by embroiderers.

Quilting has a long tradition of recording personal histories and special events. In the 1800s signature and memorial quilts were very popular. Often a special piece of fabric would be incorporated in the quilt design, which would be a poignant reminder of friends and families. These heirloom quilts were a way of transmitting family history to future generations.

Quilting is still a widely popular medium for preserving memories, for raising awareness of social issues and as commemoration for important events in contemporary history.

Above left: Antique German ecclesiastical embroidery.

Above right: Antique quilt made from coveted scraps of fabric.

Cherilyn's interpretation

Above left: Inkjet photos on cotton transfer sheet.

Above right: Laser-print heat transfer on Evolon.

Developments in techniques have influenced contemporary textiles; this is especially evident in contemporary memorial and friendship quilts. Photo transfer allows the reproduction of true images of subjects. Iron-on photo-transfer paper is readily available and allows digital images to be printed from the home printer.

Practical suggestions

- Collect a series of personal digital photos: if you have a theme to work with you can select photos around this theme. Think of the people and places that relate to your idea. Consider the colour you want to work with: what is most relevant to your theme? Full colour, monochromatic effects or even sepia tints? Using your home printer print out the images you wish to include in your work onto transfer paper.
- Decide on the sort of work you want to make. Will it be a patchwork design with printed images arranged in a pieced construction? Or would you prefer to print onto a whole-cloth base, which can be subsequently quilted or embroidered?

Above: Laser-print heat transfer on Evolon.

- Decide on the format of the prints you want to transfer. Do you want a single image on a background, or do you want to make a collage of images? In this case you can tear and arrange several images in a composition and transfer them by ironing onto your base fabric.

Another interesting option for printing your own images directly from your computer is to use ready prepared sheets of cotton, silk or organza (Jacquard). These fabrics are paper backed and easy to feed into your printer. Print them, peel from backing and sew directly into your project.

Spun bonded non-woven fabrics such as Evolon and Lutradaur offer new possibilities for creative textile work. Photos can be transferred onto these fabrics by making laser photocopies of your images and ironing them directly onto the non-woven fabric. Evolon is particularly suitable for this technique as it has a smooth surface and a densely bonded structure, which is very flexible. Colour can be added to these synthetic fabrics using transfer paint.

Explore making a collage combining transferred images and text, then quilt or embroider the piece either by hand or machine.

Above left: Preparation work.

A personal interpretation

There are many possibilities: To start with, there is the choice of recycling old textiles or using new cloth as a ground fabric. The advantage of using old fabric is that it already has history, has passed through many hands and is a living testament, which can be a delight to work with. New fabric on the other hand has no history and is a blank canvas.

I have been working with the themes of bereavement, loss and commemoration for quite some time. Vintage handkerchiefs, which were passed down through the family, seem a fitting support on which to embroider images of beloved family members. They carry entangled layers of history and memory.

The images I use are partially stitched, emphasizing the idea that memories are fragile and can easily fragment or fade. This work is an attempt to preserve both memories and much loved textiles.

Hand-embroidered portraits on handkerchiefs

- Choose a piece of vintage textiles to work with. If you are not fortunate enough to have inherited pieces, scour your local charity shops or a flea market.
- Select photos to work from. Choose an image, enlarge it to A4 size and print a copy.
- Look for a light source for tracing this photo; it can be a light box if you have one or simply use the inside of a window.

- Stick the photo with tape to the light source, taping the chosen piece of textile on top.
- Make a tracing of the principal lines with a pencil.
- You are now ready to embroider. Work with stranded embroidery cotton in your chosen colour. Decide how thick you want your lines to be; two strands for a fine line, three strands or more for a thicker line.
- Choose the stitch you prefer to work with, such as chain stitch, backstitch, running stitch or stem stitch.
- Do not begin the line of stitching with a knot. Leave about 2cm (¾in) of thread at the back of the work. When lines are completed you can work this loose thread back into the line of stitching on the reverse side of the work. In this way you have a tidy reverse, which enables it to be viewed from both sides.
- Continue to stitch until all lines are completed. You can make small adjustments to the lines as you stitch, using the original photo as a guide.
- Any pencil lines that are still visible can be erased with a fabric eraser.

If you prefer not to draw onto the surface of your work, you can make a tracing of the image on tracing paper and tack this to the surface. Embroider through the paper and when stitching is completed tear the paper away carefully. Another alternative is to draw onto the reverse side of the fabric and stitch this reverse side. If you work with backstitch, the stitch on the front side of the work will be a slightly raised stem stitch.

Left, centre and right: *Memory Cloth – Three Generations*, 30 x 30 x 3cm (12 x 12 x 1¼in), Cherilyn Martin.

A personal interpretation

The idea of recording personal memories on vintage textiles developed further with embroidering vintage clothing worn by a loved one. The portrait of a bride with red roses refers to the bridal bouquet. Loose roses embroidered onto a vintage nightgown again refer to the bride's bouquet. The needle and thread left in the work refers to the continuity of the work and of memories.

Keeping a written diary is a pastime that has existed through the centuries and across many cultures. Diaries provide an insight into the past and the customs of the day, as well as telling individual stories and preserving memories.

Left: *Disenchanted Bride #1*, 50 x 60cm (19¾ x 23½in), Cherilyn Martin. Vintage blouse, hand embroidery.

Above: *Disenchanted Bride #2*, 50 x 130cm (19¾ x 51in), Cherilyn Martin. Antique nightdress, hand embroidery.

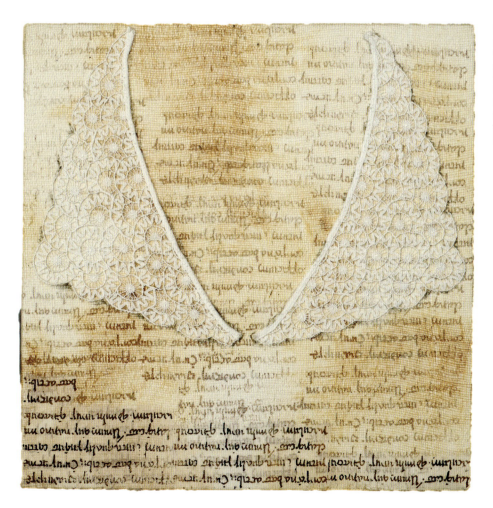

This page: *Pillow Books 1, 2* and *3*, 30 x 30 x 3cm (12 x 12 x 1¼in), Cherilyn Martin. Vintage dress collars mounted on cotton and rusted scrim with screen-printed handwritten texts.

Yesterday is History | 83

Els's interpretation

The senses

To interpret our own history all our senses can play a role:

- Smell can be a strong incentive to bring back memories; happy moments can be relived. The smell of a roast can take us back into our mother's kitchen and we are reminded of affection and warmth.
- Sound can have the same effect; we can relive happy as well as unpleasant moments.
- Touch can also take us back in time. Feeling a piece of cloth or some other textile might remind us of that little dress or a toy we once had.
- Taste – a particular taste can remind us of an earlier event, whether good or bad.
- Sight – we go through old photo albums and recall that happy, or perhaps rain-soaked, holiday and our feelings at the time.

Pay attention to simple things that are often overlooked. Something like a footstep in the sand can also be a memory; someone left his or her trace.

Memories offer an inexhaustible source of ideas. We have to choose and decide which ideas will be workable.

It is not easy to take a vague idea forward. The best thing, once again, is to write down your thoughts or to make a mind map, and be realistic about what is possible. It is better to start with a simple design and take things further from there, rather than get stuck with an idea halfway through.

Reusing an old object is also a way of giving shape to a memory. An example of this is a series of paper works that I made, *Letters from a Friend*.

Els's approach

Henk, a dear friend, died. For several decades he used to collect stamps like many other people did at that time. It was unusual, though, that he also collected envelopes. Not the valuable 'first day envelopes', but regular stamped mail.

He used to be a teacher at a village school and many parents saved their mail for 'their schoolmaster'.

Henk was an organised man; the thousands of envelopes were bundled by date, value, imagery, season etc., with everything neatly stored in boxes.

I felt it was important that his collection, which had no monetary value, should not be lost, so I took it under my wing.

Above (top): A collection of envelopes.
Above (bottom): *Letters from a Friend* (detail), Els van Baarle.

Yesterday is History | 85

Above: A piece from the series *Letters from a Friend*, 400 x 450cm (157 x 177in), Els van Baarle.

I saw it as a challenge to use this collection as a strong reminder of the friendship. To me the envelopes had tremendous sentimental value. By turning them into a series of works they would literally come to light. This precious box of envelopes thus became the series: *Letters from a Friend*.

Working in a series will stimulate your creativity. Instead of getting stuck on one idea, force yourself to ask 'What if...?' and continue from there.

Failures are experiences and also part of the work process. If you are not prepared to accept this you will not grow. Push the boundaries and choose the unpredictable, not the familiar.

The work process

- The paper of the envelopes is painted with reactive dye and then screen-printed.
- The print does not cover the original address; that had to remain visible.
- The edges are burnt and the envelopes stitched together to form long panels.
- The total work measures 4m (157in) wide x 4.5m (177in) long. About 1,000 envelopes have been used to create this work. Paper lends itself well to the same techniques that are used on fabric. The fragility of paper has a connection with the fragility of memory.

Old textiles

Like Cherilyn, I am attracted to old textiles. Old linen and cotton fabrics take dye very well and intense and deep colours can be achieved. Holes can either be darned or left as they are, becoming part of the design.

The fabric is the memory and it is being reused to be turned into a piece of art.

Suggestions for working with old textiles

Begin by examining the fabric to see what repair it needs or can withstand. Washing, dry-cleaning, airing or beating are all options. Placing the textile in the freezer for a while will kill any pests. Next, decide which techniques you would like to apply.

When choosing to work with textiles that have been embroidered, washing is not always the best choice as the colours might run. Worn fabrics can be strengthened by applying a thin cotton fabric to the back. Be wary of using fusible products; stitching a thin cotton lining will be more secure. In case the fabric is very old and valuable, it is best to ask the advice of a knowledgeable textile restorer.

An old pillowcase from a child's bed has been taken apart and dyed with Procion MX. Then it was screen-printed with textile paint and stitching was added (see right). Take a look at the back of a piece of embroidery. The thread-ends and knots often become more important than the image itself. We see only colours, textures and planes, and this could be the starting point for an idea.

Above: Recycled tablecloth, detail, 120 x 145cm (47 x 57in), Els van Baarle. Wax, dyed with Procion MX dye.

88 | Yesterday is History

Working with a specific theme

You might receive an invitation to take part in an exhibition and a certain theme is prescribed. The location of the exhibition and the prescribed theme are setting limits, but within this framework there are still lots of possibilities.

Together with the artists' group Windkracht Tien, I exhibited in the Japan Museum SieboldHuis in Leiden in the Netherlands. The work to be exhibited had to be related to Japan or the Japanese culture.

During a trip to Japan, at a temple in Tokyo, I saw appealing ways of expressing a wish; by means of little notes or small wooden labels.

As the work at the museum was going to be exhibited in an outdoor area, I decided to take the idea of the wooden labels further. The 17th-century wall, on which the work would be hung, could not be damaged by drilling holes. The wall ties could be used to hang the work on; the space in between the ties was 2m (6ft6in), so that automatically determined the width of the work. The fabric I used was old cotton, a discarded 60m (65½yd) roller towel, like those used in washrooms. This material was dyed and worked with wax using a tjap (an Indonesian copper stamp). Part of the batik wax was left in the fabric as protection against the rain. Tunnels were stitched, and into these wooden rods were inserted. The wooden wish labels were attached to these rods. The marks scribbled on the labels are made-up writing. The work is 2m (78½) wide and 4.5m(177in) long.

Left: *Counting the Days III*, 50 x 72cm (19¾ x 28¼in), Els van Baarle.

Top left: Inspiration: wooden tags outside a temple in Tokyo.

Top right: *EMA* (detail).

Above: *EMA*, 200 x 450cm (78½ x 177in), Els van Baarle. Batik on recycled cotton towels, wood.

Yesterday is History | 89

CHAPTER 6

BOOK AS OBJECT

Books play an important role in many of our lives; their content can be a window on the world and offer new insight into subjects of interest, or they can offer escapism in the form of a thriller or romantic novel. Books are tangible objects, which we take pleasure in handling, enjoying the smell of paper, studying illustrations and browsing through their contents.

Books can be inspirational to artists in various ways:

- A storyline can become a subject to develop as a theme, the artist giving their own interpretation of the story.
- A book itself can be altered by transforming its pages and cover, so that it takes on a new appearance.
- Signs of ageing or wear and tear can be inspirational. A book's worn cover or curled pages can be the starting point for a new piece of work.

People have always had the need to communicate; the evolution of the book form is fascinating, and each stage of its development offers a wealth of inspiration.

Cherilyn's interpretation

Above: *Arte Factum*, 20 x 20cm (8 x 8in), Cherilyn Martin. The clay slab as inspiration: work developed around the idea of ancient clay slabs, using marks, patterns and undecipherable text printed on hand-made paper, mounted onto a slate base.

Top right: *Scroll*, 200 x 12cm (79 x 5in), Cherilyn Martin. Collaged joss paper, Procion MX, hand stitching.

Right: *Silent Dialogue #1*, 410 x 15cm (161 x 6in), Cherilyn Martin. Silk woven band, viscose, hand stitching.

Far right: *Silent Dialogue #1* (detail), Cherilyn Martin.

Early evidence of writing is found on clay tablets from early Mesopotamian societies, where signs and characters were made in slabs of wet clay using a reed stylus. Some tablets containing important information were fired, classified and stored, while others were used for daily writing and recycled by soaking the clay and reforming the slab. When important information was sent to someone, it was wrapped in an 'envelope' of clay that protected the slab. It was subsequently broken open so that the contents could be read.

Papyrus, from which our word paper is derived, was made from the *Cyperus papyrus* plant and its first known use was in Ancient Egypt. There is evidence of its use throughout the Mediterranean region in ancient history – rolls of papyrus were discovered during early excavations of Herculaneum in the mid-18th century. Papyrus was made from the sticky pith of the plant. Once the outer skin had been stripped away, strips of pith were laid

lengthways side by side, slightly overlapping. A second layer was laid on top at right angles, and then the layers were beaten together until a single sheet was formed. After drying, the sheets were polished to create the smooth surface necessary for writing on. These sheets were often glued together to create a long strip, which was then rolled into a scroll, a familiar early book form.

This manufacturing process is described by Pliny the Elder (23–79 CE) in his work *Naturalis Historia*, an early encyclopedia written in Latin, one of the largest surviving documents of the Roman Empire.

Above: *Mourning Walk #3*, 15 x 100cm (6 x 39½in), Cherilyn Martin. Paper, mixed media and hand stitching on acrylic felt.

Book as Object | 93

a b

c d

e f

Above: Examples of leporellos (folded books), Cherilyn Martin.

94 | Book as Object

Leporellos

The term leporello derives from Mozart's opera *Don Giovanni*, in which the manservant, Leporello, reveals a register with the numerous names of his master's mistresses. This list unfolds concertina-like across the stage, emphasising the length of the list.

A leporello is a narrow length of paper or any other suitable material, which can be folded in a zig-zag fashion – otherwise known as concertina or accordion binding. This method is also found in traditional Japanese binding, orihon (or = fold, hon = book). Traditionally, Buddhists monks wrote on scrolls, however with the introduction of concertina folding their scripts were easier to handle and to store when folded in a concertina.

A leporello can vary in size from a simple two fold to a lengthy structure of multiple folds. It can be printed or worked on one or both sides, and is often used to tell or to illustrate a story. Today many artists use the leporello structure because the simple folding action turns a two-dimensional work into a free-standing independent form. This offers the challenge of a piece being viewed from all angles.

There are a few questions to ask when making a leporello:

- Is there a theme or a (visual) story to tell?
- Does what is to be depicted have a continuum through the length of the work?
- Is there a relationship between the front and back of the work?
- Do the covers reflect the content when the leporello is closed?

There are many materials available to textile artists, which are suitable for making a leporello: sturdy paper, waxed paper, reinforced fabric (e.g. stiffened, quilted etc.) or a spun bonded fabric such as Pelmet Vilene or Lutradur 130. There are also many techniques that are suitable to use, including collage, stamping, screen-printing, painting and drawing.

- Spun-bonded polyester with transfer paints, transfer rubbings, stamping with embossing powder.
- Pelmet Vilene with transfer paint, Spunfab, silk fibres, transfer foils, machine stitching.
- Paper pouches with Procion dye, screen printing with puff paste, hand tied.
- Metallic organza leporello pouches with mixed-media covers.
- Leporello stitch book, paper support, layered techniques.
- Encaustic and paper collage.

Book as Object | 95

Folding methods

Here are some examples of common folding methods used by bookbinders and graphic designers.

1. Eight-page accordion

The easiest example is to fold a long, narrow strip of paper in half and then fold the outer sides to the middle fold. You can use a bone folder to score parallel lines in the paper and to make clean creases.

2. Three-dimensional variation

This variation ensures the leporello stands sturdily: folded from a rectangular sheet of paper, a slit is cut in the middle fold, which allows the accordion to open when it is unfolded, so that images on the front and back of the papier can be seen.

3. Gate fold

Side flaps or pages are folded inwards; they can meet centrally so that the inside is hidden, resulting in a clear division between internal and external content, or the flaps can be folded more narrowly, in which case there should be a clear link between the imagery used.

4. Simple pop-up

This is the very simplest example of what is known as the 'moveable book'; examples of very complex and sophisticated constructions can be found. In its simplest form, cut-out figures can be glued to the tabs, which then pop up when the book is opened.

5. Meander folding

This structure is made from a rectangular sheet of paper, which is first divided into eight sections. A slit is made

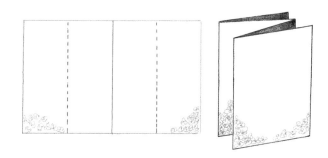

1

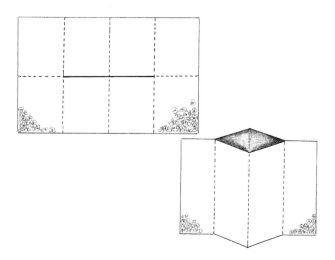

2

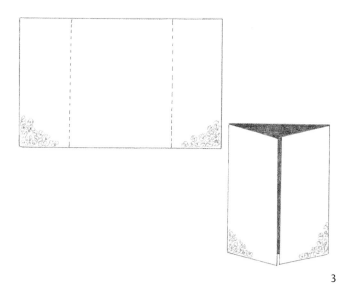

3

96 | Book as Object

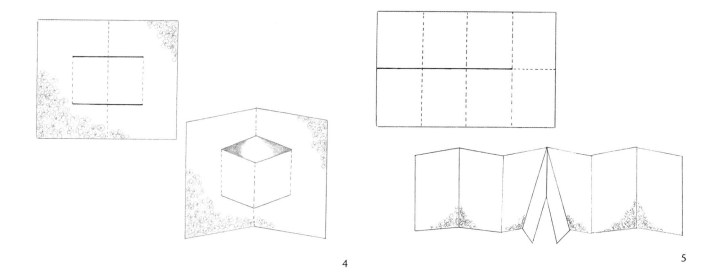

4 5

through the lengthwise crease until the last segment. Pick up one section and fold along each crease line in a concertina fashion around the entire sheet of paper.

Challenge – a step into three dimensions

Everyone has a story to tell, whether it is purely visual or written, or takes on the form of an illustrated narrative.

Choose a simple leporello with which to tell your story. Which materials do you prefer to work with? Remember it must be sturdy enough to keep its shape. (See examples a–f on page 94.) Consider the techniques that are most suitable to use with your chosen material. At this stage you can decide whether it will be purely decorative or if you have a message to convey. Remember that you are now faced with the challenge of the work being seen from all angles. The 'back' should also make a statement and have as much impact as the 'front'. Both sides should be complementary and not vie for attention.

A leporello is also a great way of presenting any sampling you may have done (see example e). You have the choice of mounting a strip of worked samples onto the folded background or to attach individual pieces to each 'page' of the leporello. You could even make a folded structure with pouches, so that pieces can be saved inside the pockets (see a, c and d).

Book objects as inspiration

Above: Old, worn books can be inspiration.

Above right: *Book #4*, Cherilyn Martin. In this work the top 'page' has been lined with an embossed copper sheet.

Apart from its content or storyline, the book itself can be a source of inspiration for new work. The character of a newly printed book soon changes as it is handled by a string of readers. Corners are often turned, notes are made on pages and phrases underlined; gradually the book becomes worn and torn. Look in your own book collection for a book with signs of ageing. A secondhand bookshop is also a great source, full of books revealing physical signs of wear and tear.

Examine an old book and consider which elements would be interesting to interpret in fabric, paper or mixed media. A simple row of books on a shelf can be fascinating; bookspines are sometimes decorative, have embossed gold lettering or elaborate typefaces. Even the repetition of the spines is interesting.

Lay an old book on a table and examine the curves of the open book and the way the pages turn, or see what happens when pages turn in on themselves to make repeated curves.

It is fascinating how interesting turned corners of pages can be; they are sometimes creased by the reader or just curl over from constant use. Shown left is a work made in response to these worn corners.

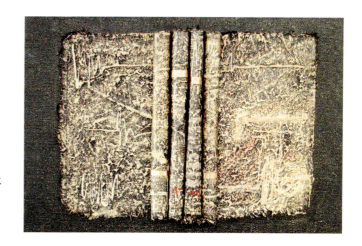

Above: *Book #1*, detail, Cherilyn Martin. Work based on the repetitive element of book spines. Textural paper has been painted with black Procion dye, then rubbed with a metallic paintstick so that the texture of the paper becomes more evident. Copper strips have been added and hand stitching, which suggest lettering.

Right: *Pages #1*, 20 x 20 x 3cm (8 x 8 x 1¼in), Cherilyn Martin. This work, inspired by turned pages, is made from fused sheets of plastic, with Spunfab, Angelina fibres and oil paint trapped in the layers and with fusible film laminated on the surface. Text has been screen-printed on top.

Book as Object | 99

Els's interpretation

Throughout the centuries it has been commonplace to reuse all kinds of materials: building bricks, tools, clothing, bed linen and furniture; repairing and reusing was a normal phenomenon. Famous painters also used the backs of their paintings, or they applied a new layer of paint on top of an existing image.

In medieval times monks would use parchment for their books and manuscripts. This is a thin, paper-like material, made from animal hide. This parchment, too, was reused by scratching away old texts and applying new ones.

It has only been over the last few decades that the Western world has become a 'consumer society'. Today, we are trying to reduce wastefulness in all kinds of ways.

Papermaking and recycling

Before 1850 paper was made from rags: cotton, linen, hemp and burlap were the most important raw materials. Paper was produced in wind- or water-powered mills.

The rags were sorted, cleaned and cut into small pieces by women and children. Then this material was ground into fibres by the paper mill.

These fibres were mixed with water into a pulp. This pulp was scooped up with a flat, rectangular sieve. The surplus water would drain off and the fibres would stick together and form a sheet of paper. This sheet of paper had to be removed carefully from the sieve. It was then pressed between layers of felt and left to dry.

Papermaking has been a manual craft for a very long time. Old books often have frayed edges, which are typical for hand-made papers. When this old paper is used to make new work, the frayed edges will give it an extra dimension. Hand-made paper looks different to contemporary industrially produced paper. This old material is nice to the touch, and has character. It is a wonderful ground for printing. Old books, even old bibles, can serve as the basis for new work.

The thin pages of old books are smooth because of the process of calendering. In this process the paper is flattened by pressing it between two rollers. This smoothness makes it a little more difficult for the paper to absorb ink or dye.

Working with wax and dye

Another use for old paper is to alter it with batik wax and dye, resulting in a complete transformation. The text on the pages can either be left legible or made to disappear altogether. Individual pages can be taken from the book or the book can be used as a whole.

Above: Tools for working with wax. The newspaper on the right has lines of wax applied with a tjanting.

Method of working

Working with wax is a resist technique. The parts of the paper that are covered with wax will not absorb the dye and thus will be left uncoloured. The wax makes the paper translucent. Depth can be created by repeating the different steps of wax and dye.

You will need:

- wax pot with a thermostat
- 50/50 mixture of beeswax and paraffin
- tjanting or brushes
- Procion MX dye, ink, watercolour paint etc.

How to proceed:

- Cover your table with a plastic sheet.
- Heat the wax to 70–75°C. Start with the lowest temperature.
- When the wax is too hot it will be difficult to control and will spread too much. When this happens, the fastest way to cool it down is to add more wax. You should always prevent the wax from becoming so hot that it starts to smoke.
- When the wax is the right temperature you must decide which part or parts of the page to cover with wax. On thin paper the wax will penetrate right through to the back and both

Above: Wax and dye on antique paper from 1790, 10 x 15cm (4 x 6in), Els van Baarle.

sides of the paper will be identical. The wax will usually not penetrate thick paper, but it will still work as a resist.

- You can make fine lines using a tjanting; this is a pen-like tool with a little reservoir to hold the wax.
- Where the wax is applied over text the paint or dye will be resisted in these places. The paper will remain white and the text will be left legible. This way, parts of the text can be emphasised.
- The paper can be coloured by using ink, watercolour paint, diluted acrylic paint or Procion MX fibre-reactive dye. In the latter case the Procion powder is mixed in water, without adding salt or soda, as is done for dyeing fabric.
- The colours of the reactive dyes are intense and transparent. Each layer of colour will mix with the one underneath. Start with lighter colours first; dark colours are usually the last step, as they are difficult to over-dye. Sometimes the dye will penetrate the paper and also colour the back, depending on the thickness of the paper.

Above: *Novum Testamentum Latine*, 15 x 850cm (6 x 335in), Els van Baarle. Wax and dye.

Removing the wax

- Cover your ironing board with a stack of newspaper sheets, either printed or blank. If you use printed newspaper, it must be older than four weeks, otherwise the print may transfer onto your work.
- Set your iron to 'cotton'. Put one sheet of newspaper on top of your work and slowly iron over the paper for the excess wax to be absorbed.
- Some of the wax is left in the work and an interesting transparency will be the result.
- The wax will also make the paper stiffer and stronger, which can be useful when working with very thin paper.

Transforming a bible

For the piece shown above, an antique bible was taken apart. Each page was then treated with layers of wax and dye. After removing the excess wax, the pages were placed slightly overlapping onto a fabric base (in this case a kind of tulle). They were attached to the base fabric by fusing with Bondaweb. The last step was to add a layer of screen-printed text.

Found objects and books

Sometimes you will find an object with an intriguing shape. Such an object can be the starting point for a book project.

The first step will be to study the object from all sides. In doing so, use your eyes, as well as your hands:

- What does the object feel like: is it smooth, light, heavy?
- Which materials and techniques would be suitable to use in combination with the object?
- How can you ensure that the basic shape and the added materials have unity?

Then ask the following questions:

- Do you see certain lines and planes in the object?
- Should these lines/planes be followed or ignored?
- Which should be the most important part?
- Which materials and techniques will suit the object?
- When is a book a book?
- Can just two pages form a book?
- Is text required?
- How will it be presented?

Below: Barrel-organ book, wax, dye, silkscreen, 23 x 330cm (9 x 130in), Els van Baarle.

It is not just found objects that can form the starting point for a piece of work. Inspiration could, for instance, also be found in outdoor observations.

Above: 10 x 15cm (4 x 6in), Els van Baarle.

Below: Wax, dye, discharge and print on cotton, 15 x 30cm (6 x 12in), Els van Baarle.

Top: Detail of a building destroyed by fire was the inspiration for the work below.

Above: Old hinge, wax and dye on hand-made paper 20 x 30cm (8 x 12in). This old hinge has elements that remind us of medieval times. The work reflects the atmosphere of that period, Els van Baarle.

Book as Object | 105

Below: Wood, transparent fabric, dye and silkscreen, metallic paint. Interesting shapes of wood have been used as a support for a new book object. 15 x 15cm (6 x 6in) and 10 x 10cm (4 x 4in), Els van Baarle.

Above: Wooden base, old book pages, wax and dye. 7 x 10 x 5cm (2½ x 4 x 2in), Els van Baarle.

Below: Wax, paint, silkscreen, stitch on synthetic fabric, 20 x 95cm (8 x 37½in), Els van Baarle.

Right: *Poem*, 30 x 90cm (12 x 35½in), Els van Baarle. Wax, dye and print on cotton.

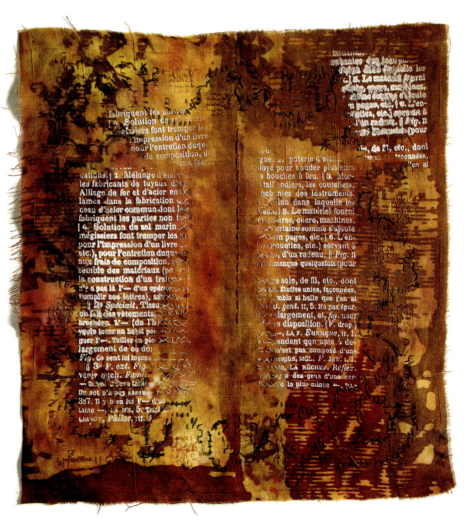

Below: An old manuscript was used as inspiration for this work. 35 x 35cm (13¾ x 13¾in), Els van Baarle.

Book as Object | 107

CHAPTER 7

ARTICLES IN EVERYDAY USE

This book contains several photos that were taken in different countries. It is a known fact that anything unusual to us draws our attention. The colourful display of exotic fruit and vegetables on a Japanese market immediately has to be photographed. Architecture in a foreign country, practical objects previously unknown to us, anything that's different and never seen before – all these things make us curious.

Something which is new to us, seems to be easier to translate into creative work. However, it is a misconception that we need to travel to far away places to find inspiration.

Looking, then seeing

We constantly use our eyes; we look, but ultimately see (perceive) very little. Learn to analyse – it is a step towards looking creatively and designing. In this way you can discover the riches of the world which surround you, in particular when they are nearby.

This is a world filled with shapes and colours that encourage us to create. Everybody has the capacity to discover; the familiar environment of one's own home offers countless possibilities. The challenge lies in letting yourself be amazed by the ordinary.

Art does not reproduce what we see. It makes us see.
Paul Klee

A journey through the home

How many times have you opened your front door? Would you know, without checking, precisely what the doorknob looks like? With how many screws has it been attached? Would you be able to draw the doorknob from memory? Try this and then see whether you have got it right. Going through the door, you will probably enter the space where your coat rack is. In which ways have the coats been hung? A piece of clothing on a coat hanger has different folds and shadows than a coat on a hook.

- Take photos as if it is the first time you see this. Be surprised, as if you have entered a different culture.
- Print a photo and accentuate the shadow lines with a marker; does this result in interesting surface patterns?
- Do not just use your eyes; the sense of touch is an elementary means of getting to know an object. Does it have texture? Does the surface evoke an emotion?

We travel further, into the kitchen. This is a place where we can find most things blindfolded. Look at how things are arranged, is it tidy or perhaps disorderd? Are the dishes stacked according to their size, from large to small? Are the cups and glasses sorted?

Go through your kitchen drawer, what is in it? The drawer is a real treasury.

Above: *Souvenir de ma Jeunesse*, 18 x 450cm (7 x 177in), Els van Baarle. Handwoven cotton, collage, hand-stitched and partially printed with a wooden block with glued-on matches.

Articles in Everyday Use | 111

Some suggestions for projects

Explore the shapes and possibilities of the following items:

- corkscrew
- elastic bands
- paperclips
- knives, forks, spoons
- can opener
- matchboxes and matches
- empty cans
- cookie cutters
- potato masher
- rolling pin
- baking tins
- packaging

Els's interpretation

Playing with objects from the kitchen

Play becomes joy, joy becomes work, work becomes play.
Johannes Itten

- Choose a simple object, such as a fork. On a piece of paper, draw the fork with your eyes closed. Now draw it again with the other hand. Then draw it with three marker pens tied together and watch how the lines are randomly interrupted.
- Cut up one or more of these drawings into 3cm (1¼in) squares. Arrange them into an abstract image. This could be the starting point for an appliqué, embroidery or screen-printing.
- The fork can be used to print with, using textile paint; it can be made into a stamp, using mouldable foam or dipped into hot batik wax and printed onto fabric or paper as a resist for dye or paint. A simple fork, drawn with your eyes closed, can lead to diverse pieces of artwork.

Left: Copies of a fork drawing have been cut up and rearranged. A thermofax screen was made of this new image. Els van Baarle.

Right: Several screen-prints with textile paint. The background is a synthetic fabric, coloured with transfer dyes. Els van Baarle.

Right: 25 x 30cm (10 x 12in), Els van Baarle. Overlapping prints using the same motif on cotton, worked with batik wax. The fork has become an abstract shape. The scratches in the wax, together with the print, give the impression of graffiti. Textile paint on wax and Procion MX dye.

Articles in Everyday Use | 113

More suggestions for projects

Make two still lives using various kitchen utensils. Arrange the objects into a symmetrical and an asymmetrical composition (see page 20).

- Take photos of these compositions to see the differences between the two.
- Other variations of contrast could be large/small, order/disorder, many/few.
- Print a photo and draw the main lines or only the shadows. Could you use this pattern?
- Choose a more complicated object and turn it upside down. Take a photo, then try to render the object in simple line drawings.

Left: Organic print on silk and cotton, using spaghetti, tomato, French bean, courgette and rice glued to a wooden block, as well as feathers. 25 x 95cm (10 x 37½in).

Food as a tool

Food can be used as a tool, too, without having to waste any of it. There are often parts of a food that we do not eat and which can be used as a stamp.

We probably all remember the potato prints we made in primary school. Sprouted potatoes, unfit for consumption, could be used for this. Professional results can be achieved, especially when several overlapping prints are made.

Making a stamp

Many objects can be used for printing by fixing them to a wooden block. To do so, cover the wood with strong, double-sided carpet tape. To prevent the edges of the wooden block being printed, stick the tape right up to the sides and attach your object to it. When attaching several objects to the wood, make sure they are all of the same height and leave some space in between them. Use a paint roller to apply paint to the stamp for an even distribution of paint.

Above: Handmade stamps – plastic numbers, foam, string, tractor tyre inner tube, wooden puzzle pieces and upholstery have been attached to wooden blocks with strong double-sided tape.

Inspiration is everywhere

Kitchen utensils and food can be inspiration for your work, but you can also look at other everyday objects, for instance, a toddler's chair. Basically, inspiration can be anywhere – first you have to look, and then you have to see.

Chair

Study the object from all sides, as if you had never seen it before. We will use a chair as an example:

• With different media – felt-tip pen, ink, large brush, fine brush – draw a line without lifting the drawing implement from the paper (continuous line).

• Make a positive as well as a negative drawing (draw the background only, leaving a blank space for where the chair is).

• Make photocopies of your drawings in several sizes, or use a photo-editing program on your computer. The subject can become abstract by using just a detail of it.

Left: A detail of a drawing was enlarged and used for this screen-print on silk. Textile paint on silk, coloured with Procion MX dye. Els van Baarle. 90 x 225cm (35½ x 88½in).

Above left: Detail of a black-and-white drawing of a chair used to print the textile shown left.

Below: Several prints were made with the thermofax screen shown right, 90 x 140cm (35 x 55in), Els van Baarle. Cotton, dyed with Procion MX dye, printed with textile paint.

Right: Thermofax screen made from a sketch of a chair.

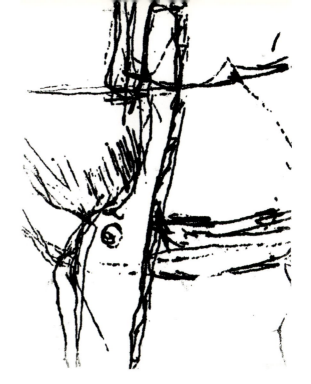

Articles in Everyday Use | 117

Right: *Memory Cloth #5*, detail, Cherilyn Martin. A German 'Paradekissen', (a large antique decorative pillowcase), featuring rust dyeing, controlled rusting, screen-printing and machine stitching.

Cherilyn's interpretation

Textiles play a major role in our daily lives, even if they are taken for granted by many. Clothing protects us from the elements, blankets keep us warm, soft furnishings add comfort and ambience to our homes. This has been true of all cultures throughout the centuries.

Over the years I have built up a collection of antique domestic textiles which I occasionally handle and examine, but for the rest they are stored out of sight.

I have chosen to work with this collection, to give these pieces of textiles new life and the chance to be admired by a wider public.

A great responsibility however and a challenge: how to preserve the integrity of these old textiles and at the same time add one's own input.

Giving new life to old textiles

Vintage textiles are fabrics with history – they have a story to tell. They often show signs of wear and tear; stains and discolouring are commonplace and are evidence of their extensive use in a domestic setting.

When using these pieces as a support on which to tell one's own story, it is essential that the textile piece retains its own identity.

Left: *Memory Cloth #6*, 180 x 90cm (71 x 35½in), Cherilyn Martin. An Italian vintage pillowcase with white work embroidered inserts, unpicked to show piece in its entirety. Rust dyeing, controlled rusting, screen-printing, machine stitching.

How to start

If you are lucky enough to have inherited some textile pieces, you could think about how you can add something that reflects your life, such as a poem, information about the family or special events. If these textiles are too precious to use, search thrift shops or secondhand markets for vintage pieces.

As discussed before, creating new work entails making a series of decisions. When embarking on new work we rely on the myriad of techniques acquired and in-depth knowledge of the media we use. We must also use intuition and take risks in order to break new ground.

'Risk taking' can certainly be applied to the rust-dyeing technique, as its outcome is often random and difficult to predict; even so, the results are often surprising and delightful. It is possible to achieve sharp images or patterning depending on the rusted objects you use. Individual prints of a chosen object can also be made, depending on the effects you require. The process is an ideal way to cover the stains vintage textiles have acquired with time, which are often very difficult to remove and stop us from using them in our homes.

It is advisable to make several sample pieces before embarking on a project using precious fabrics or unique vintage textiles. You will then have more of an idea of what the outcome might be and what is achievable.

You must always be prepared for mishaps and be armed with solutions to save the piece. When a rust stain is disappointing, you can work into it with a combination of surface design techniques to alter its appearance. For instance, screen-printing with a similarly coloured textile paint, stamping and embroidery are all effective methods, worked in layers so that the stain becomes less dominant and more integrated.

Rust dyeing

Materials and equipment required:

- pieces of rusty metal
- fabric (cotton, linen, silk)
- white vinegar
- spray bottle
- salt
- plastic tray
- 2 plastic buckets

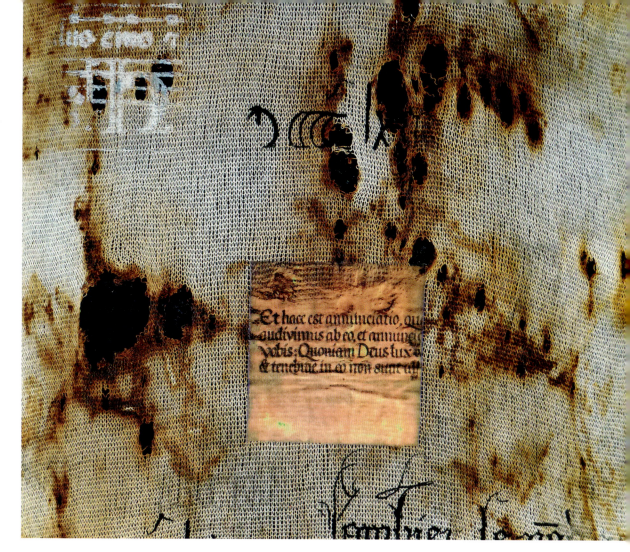

Right: *It's the Stones that Speak #VII*, 120 x 200cm (47 x 78¾in), Cherilyn Martin. Fine cotton tricot, random rust dyeing showing signs of rust decay. Screen printing with puff paint and textile paint.

Process:

- Soak or spray your fabric with a solution of vinegar and water.
- Place the fabric on a plastic tray and place rusted objects on top. You can also wrap the objects with the fabric. For full contact, weigh down with a heavy object.
- Keep spraying the fabric over a short period of time until the rust is activated.
- After a day or two the fabric will be stained. The longer you leave the fabric the deeper the colour will become.
- When using silk or fine cotton, note that the fabric will begin to disintegrate after a few days. (This can be interesting for a project on a theme of decay.)
- When rusting is completed, wash the fabric in a bucket with warm water mixed with a small amount of salt. This stops the rusting process and fixes the rust.
- Wash again in a bucket of warm, soapy water.

Safety: Whichever rusting technique you use, make sure you wear rubber gloves to avoid any skin contact with rust, wear protective clothing and a mask suitable for protection against inhaling fine particles (iron ore).

Controlled rusting technique

This controlled rusting technique enables you to use stencils or screen-prinrted letters or images to place rusty elements precisely. It requires rusting powder and a medium such as acrylic wax.

Top: Materials for controlled rusting: paper stencil with text, vintage altar cloth, acrylic wax and rusting powder.

Bottom: The altar cloth shown above during the rusting process.

Materials needed:

- fabric
- acrylic wax
- rusting powder
- freezer paper
- foam roller
- plastic plate
- letter shapes to draw around (there are plenty of alphabets available in craft shops)
- white vinegar
- spray bottle
- salt
- sharp craft knife
- cutting board
- pencil
- ruler
- rubber gloves
- apron
- mask
- 2 plastic buckets

Process:

First, refer to the safety instructions on page 121. This is a messy technique so protect working surfaces and the floor with plastic sheeting. Don't work outside on a windy day unless protected from the wind.

- Decide on the size of the text you wish to add to your work and cut a piece of freezer paper 10cm (4in) larger in width and height.
- Choose the letters you need for your text from your chosen alphabet. Draw a guideline on the freezer paper with a pencil and draw around the shapes.
- When your text is complete, cut out the lettering with a sharp craft knife, protecting the working surface with a cutting board.
- Iron the freezer paper carefully onto the fabric.
- Roll out some acrylic wax onto a plastic plate with the foam roller.
- Carefully roll the acrylic wax onto the freezer-paper stencil, making sure all the open shapes are covered.
- At this point you need your rubber gloves, apron and mask. Sprinkle rusting powder carefully over the stencil, making sure you do not use

122 | Articles in Everyday Use

Above: *Memory Cloth #6* (detail), Cherilyn Martin.

too much or it may spread over the uncovered surface of the fabric.

- Shake off the surplus rusting powder from your work onto a spare piece of plastic and remove from the working area. This surplus rusting powder can be returned to its container and used again.
- Spray white vinegar onto the area of lettering, taking care not to overdo it. The rest of the fabric should remain dry, so that there is no chance of fine particles of rusting powder rusting on other areas of your fabric.
- Leave to dry. Rusting should begin within an hour or so, depending on the temperature of the environment. If things dry out quickly before rusting begins, spray again.
- When you are satisfied that rusting has occurred and the work is dry, remove the freezer paper from the fabric.
- Wash the fabric in a bucket of warm water with some salt. You may need to scrub the lettering with a nail brush to remove the encrusted powder. The residue should sink to the bottom of the bucket.
- Remove and wash carefully once or twice in a clean bucket with warm, soapy water.
- Dry and iron the fabric.

When you are satisfied with the rusting you have done, you can think about ways you could integrate the results into the work. Think about the idea you are trying to convey, and add more details to enrich the surface. Screen-printing, block printing and embroidery are all possible.

Materials

Dyes and paints

Wear gloves and a mask when handling powders; work in a well-ventilated area. For every material, read the instructions from the supplier.

Many of the artworks in this book are coloured with dyes and paints. There are several good books available about using dyes, paints etc., and advice can also be found on the internet. Be careful however, as there is also incorrect information around.

Fabric paint and printing ink

Fabric paints and printing inks can be applied to every kind of fabric, including most of the synthetics. Depending on the consistency of the paint you have chosen, you can print, silkscreen or make watercolour washes. Fabric paint covers the top of the fabric and may affect the feel of the fabric. Follow the supplier's instructions for how to set the paints.

Dye

Dye makes a bond with the fibre. Procion MX fibre-reactive dye can be used on all natural fibres, such as cotton, linen, rayon, silk, paper, etc.

Cellulose fibres need soda ash or washing soda to fix the dye in the fibre. Dye can also be used on wool and protein fibre, but not with the cotton method.

There are many different dyeing techniques, from hand painting and shibori to tub dyeing etc.

Dye can be used with a thickener for silk-screening, printing and hand painting where you want a controlled result.

As always, follow the supplier's instructions.

Acid dyes

Acid dyes give very vivid colours on protein fibres, such as silk and wool.

As always, follow the supplier's instructions.

Transfer dyes or disperse dyes

Transfer and disperse dyes are available as powder as well as in a thickened version. They will work well on synthetic fabric and nonwovens. The colours are bright, light and wash-fast.

An interesting way of using transfer dye is to hand-paint or print on paper and iron these papers onto synthetic fabric or a non-woven. Although the painted paper looks dull, the result on the fabric is bright.

Wax

A variety of waxes are available for different surface-design techniques. There are several different ways of using hot wax, but the most important thing is to use a safe, thermostatically controlled pot. Always start at a low temperature and check if the wax is penetrating the fabric.

- **Beeswax** is a strong, flexible resist and can be mixed with paraffin for more crackle.
- **Batik wax** is often made from paraffin and sticky wax, as a substitute for beeswax.
- **Soy wax** is a fume-free alternative to oil-based waxes. It can be easily removed from fabric with a hot wash (60°C).

Tools that can be used with wax include brushes, stamps that can stand the heat, tjaps (traditional Indonesian copper blocks) and tjantings for wax drawing.

Silkscreen

The traditional tool for silkscreening is a wooden or metal frame with a polyester screen material attached. There are different screens available for textile work or for working on paper. You can make your own screens, but you must ensure that you attach the screen material as tightly as possible.

Images can be made with a photographic emulsion, but there are many other simple ways to use your screen as a tool for experimenting and playing.

You can experiment with:
- masking fluid
- masking tape (can be attached to the screen but also to the fabric)
- freezer paper
- crayon rubbings
- different kind of resists, such as flour paste
- hot wax, cold wax
- discharge paste
- foil glue

Thermofax screening process

With a thermofax screen machine it is easy to make a screen with your own image. Screens are made using a heat and light process. The screen material is fed with a laser-print copy of artwork through the thermofax machine, the plastic film burns away and the fine detailed screen is ready.

As always, follow the supplier's instructions.

Spunbonded/non-woven fabrics

Spunbonded/non-woven fabrics are made from polymer filaments. Several of these synthetic fabrics have been featured in work in this book, including Lutradur and Evolon. Transfer paint and crayons are used to colour these synthetic fabrics, as described above. They are heat sensitive, and a textile soldering iron can be used to draw into the surfaces or to cut out shapes. A heat gun can be used to distort the surface of the fabric.

Transfer foils

Transfer foils, which are available in a wide range of colours, are suitable for use on fabric and some papers. They can be used to add metallic highlights to the surface of the work. They can be heat-transferred onto fabric/paper with double-sided adhesives, such as Bondaweb or Spunfab/ Fuse FX. Transfer foil glue is also available and can be used for screen-printing, stamping and free-hand painting; transfer foil is ironed onto the print using baking paper for protection. Bonding powder and Hotspots are also adhesives that can be used with foils.

Rusting powder

Rusting powder is an iron-ore powder which can be used for rusting purposes. After stamping or screen-printing with acrylic wax onto fabric or paper, rusting powder is sprinkled over the surface and sprayed with vinegar to initiate the rusting process. Fabric can then be washed to remove the dried rusted crust; the surface of paper can be carefully scraped to remove it. Always wear a mask and protective clothing for this technique.

Wireform

Wireform is a mesh made from aluminium that can be sandwiched between layers of paper and fabric. This enables the work to be moulded into shape, and the surface can be distorted or three-dimensional shapes formed. The sandwiched layers can then be stitched by hand or machine.

Puff paint or Xpandaprint

Puff paint or Xpandaprint paint can be applied to fabric and paper. These can be used in screen-printing, stamping, stencilling and free-hand painting. When heated with a heat gun it expands and creates a raised effect on the surface. Xpandaprint is available in white and black, or colour can be mixed into the paint before use. However, it is safer to paint the raised surface with acrylic or textile paint after the paint has been 'puffed', to avoid any fumes that may be released during heating.

Suppliers

Suppliers for dyes, chemicals and paints

KEMTEX EDUCATIONAL SUPPLIES
Carrs Industrial Estate
Haslington
Rossendale
Lancashire
UK
www.kemtex.co.uk
enquiries@regencyfcb.com

DHARMA TRADING CO.
1805 South McDowell Boulevard Ext.
Petaluma,
Ca 94954
USA
www.dharmatrading.com
service@dharmatrading.com

PRO CHEMICAL & DYE
126 Shove St.
Fall River, MA 02724
USA
www.prochemicalanddye.net

JACQUARD PRODUCTS
Rupert, Gibbon & Spider Inc.
P.O.Box 425
Healdsburg,
Ca 95448
USA
www.jacquardproducts.com
service@jacquardproducts.com

BATIK OETORO
3/11 Nevin Close,
Gateshead, NSW 2290
Australia
www.dyeman.com
sales@dyeman.com

KRAFTKOLOUR
P.O.Box 379,
Whittlesea, Vic 3757
Australia
www.kraftkolour.net.au

Specialist Textile, Craft and Art suppliers

VYCOMBE ARTS AT ART VAN GO
The Studios
1 Stevenage Road
Knebworth
Hertfordshire SG3 6AN
UK
www.vycombe-arts.co.uk
www.artvango.co.uk
art@artvango.co.uk

GEORGE WEIL & SONS LTD
Old Portsmouth Road
Peasmarsh
Guildford
Surrey GU3 1LZ
UK
www.georgeweil.com
esales@georgeweil.com

RAINBOW SILKS
6 Wheelers Yard
High Street
Great Missenden
Buckinghamshire HP16 OAL
UK
www.rainbowsilks.co.uk
caroline@rainbowsilks.co.uk

LTC-LEIDEN B.V.
W. Barentszstraat 11-13
2315 TZ Leiden
Netherlands
www.ltcleiden.nl
info@ltcleiden.nl

ZIJDELINGS
Kapelstraat 93A 5046 CL
Tilburg
Netherlands
www.zijdelings.eu
kvvught@zijdelings.com

MIJN-EIGEN.NL
Gestelsestraat 238
5654AM Eindhoven
Netherlands
www.mijn-eigen.nl
info@mijn-eigen.nl

STOF TOT VERVEN
Fien de la Marstraat 10
3207 VG Spijkenisse
www.stoftotverven.nl
info@stoftotverven.nl

Further Reading

BOOKS ON COLOUR

Josef Albers, *Interaction of Color* (Yale University Press, 2013)

Eva Heller, *Wie Farben wirken* (Rowohlt Verlag GmbH, 2004)

Ellen Marx, *Contrast of Colors* (Van Nostrand Reinhold, 1974)

Ellen Marx, *Optical Color and Simultaneity* (Van Nostrand Reinhold, 1983)

John Gage, *Colour and Culture* (Thames and Hudson, 1995)

Johannes Itten, *The Elements of Color* (Van Nostrand Reinhold, 1971)

Johanns Itten, *The Art of Color* (Van Nostrand Reinhold, 1974)

BOOKS ON DYEING

Kate Wells, *Fabric Dyeing & Printing* (Conran Octopus, 1997)

Joanna Kinnersly-Taylor, *Dyeing and Screen-Printing on Textiles*
   (A & C Black, 2003)

Elin Noble, *Dyes and Paints* (That Patchwork Place, 1998)

Ann Johnston, *Colour by Design: Paint and Print with Dye*
   (Ann Johnston, 2001)

QUILT, EMBROIDERY AND DESIGN RELATED READING:

Ruth Issett, *Glorious Papers* (Batsford, 2001)

Julia Caprara, *Exploring Colour* (d4daisy Books, 2008)

Janet Twinn, *Colour in Art Quilts* (Batsford, 2011)

Gwen Hedley, *Surfaces for Stitch* (Batsford, 2000)

Gwen Hedley, *Drawn to Stitch* (Batsford 2010)

Jan Beany and Jean Littlejohn, *Stitch Magic* (Batsford, 1998)

Steven Aimone, *Design! A Lively Guide to Design Basics for Artists
   & Craftspeople* (Lark Books, 2004)

Ann Johnston, *The Quilter's Book of Design Second Edition*
   (Ann Johnston, 2008)

WEBSITES:

Mind-mapping: www.imindmap.com

www.stolpersteine.eu

Index

Accordion binding 95, 96

Antique 77, 103, 118

Bayeux tapestry 76

Block printing 114, 115

Bondaweb 48, 52, 103, 124

Composition 18, 19, 20, 21, 26, 79

Controlled rusting 122, 124

Crazy quilting 77

Demnig, Gunter 38

Dye 24, 35, 55, 100 ,101, 102, 124

Drawing 16, 73, 80, 95, 112

Encaustic 19, 55, 69, 95, 96

Embroidery 35, 76, 77, 112

Evolon 43, 78, 79, 124

Embossing 95

Focal point 19, 20, 21

Folding methods 5, 96, 97

Fibonacci 18

Graffiti 52, 53, 113

Gravestones 30, 33, 34, 35, 42

Golden mean 18

Hand stitching 48, 76, 80, 81, 82

Inkjet prints 78, 79

Inspiration 12, 15 ,16,17,31, 46, 48, 65, 76, 92, 110, 116

Itten, Johannes 22, 112, 126

Journey 9, 46, 110

Kitchen 84, 112, 114, 116

Laser prints 78, 79, 124

Leporello 94, 95

Mark-making 17

Non wovens 43, 124

Opus anglicanum 77

Old textiles 76,80, 82

Pompeii 60, 61

Portraits 80, 81, 82

Procion mx dye 35, 52, 68, 88, 95, 124

Puff paint 26, 95

Proportion 18

Quilting 72, 73, 77

Rubbing 31, 32, 34, 36, 40, 41, 43, 52, 72

Rubbing plates 43

Rust dyeing 120, 121

Screen printing 118, 119

Spunfab 48, 49, 99

Stamps 115, 124

Shape 16, 18, 19, 30, 47, 84, 97, 110, 112

Senses 84

Stencil 53, 55, 122, 125

Tags 55

Thermofax screening process 124

Transfer dyes 43, 113, 124

Transfer paper 78

Trapunto 42

Vintage 80, 82, 118, 120

Wax 9, 35, 55, 68, 89, 95, 101, 102, 105, 112, 113

Acknowledgements and picture credits

Our sincere thanks go to:

Tina Persaud at Pavilion Books for giving us the opportunity to make this wonderful book.

Marie-Therese Wisniowsky for writing the foreword and for her support.

Meta Heemskerk for the translation of Els van Baarle's texts..

All photography by Joop van Houdt, except the following:

Rob Martin: pages 98 & 99.

Els van Baarle & Cherilyn Martin, all inspiration photos used throughout the book.